MW01517792

LEAVEN
REVEALED

"Good or bad – a little leaven leavens the whole lump."

BOOKS BY MICHAEL SCANTLEBURY

Five Pillars of The Apostolic

Apostolic Purity

Apostolic Reformation

Kingdom Advancing Prayer Volume I

Kingdom Advancing Prayer Volume II

Kingdom Advancing Prayer Volume III

Internal Reformation

God's Nature Expressed Through His Names

Jesus Christ The Apostle and High Priest of Our Profession

"I Will Build My Church." – Jesus Christ

Identifying and Defeating The Jezebel Spirit

Available from Publishers: Word Alive www.wordalive.ca

LEAVEN REVEALED

"Good or bad – a little leaven leavens the whole lump."

MICHAEL SCANTLEBURY

Michael Scantlebury has taken *author's prerogative* in capitalizing certain words that are not usually capitalized according to standard grammatical practice. Also, please note that the name satan and related names are not capitalized as we choose not to acknowledge him, even to the point of disregarding standard grammatical practice.

LEAVEN REVEALED
ISBN 978-1-77069-108-7

Legal Deposit – Library and Archives of Canada, 2010

Published by: Word Alive Press – www.wordalivepress.ca

Editorial Consultant: Anita Thompson – 604-521-6042

Cover design by: Michelle Soon – 604-789-9746

Printed in Canada.

Mixed Sources
Cert no. SW-COC-001271
© 1996 FSC
FSC

LEAVEN REVEALED

DEDICATION

This book is dedicated first of all to the Apostle and High Priest of my confession, Jesus Christ. I am truly grateful to Him, for by His Holy Spirit He has granted me the Grace to write this book. More specifically it is dedicated to my wife Sandra for her tireless support and commitment to God's purpose. To our children, the leadership and the tremendous family of Believers here at Dominion-Life International Ministries who have been standing strong with us in the ministry. They understood as I spent countless hours writing this book.

This book is also dedicated to the champions and bastion of Present Truth [2 Peter 1:12], in the Church of our Lord Jesus Christ who have stood for the pure, unadulterated truth of God's Word. Those who have not succumbed to the many types of spiritual leaven that have become prevalent in the earth and have found their way into the Church!

LEAVEN REVEALED

ENDORSEMENTS

As the New Apostolic Reformation matures, one of the greatest challenges is to keep the movement pure. Godliness and righteousness must prevail against all perverse attacks of the enemy. In an attempt to fulfill his purposes, satan frequently uses vicious and subtle infusions of ungodly leaven. We are indebted to Apostle Michael Scantlebury for this book, which deeply analyzes and exposes evil leaven of many kinds, but then ends up with a joyful and victorious revelation of the Leaven of the Kingdom. I love this book!

C. Peter Wagner, Apostolic Ambassador
Global Spheres, Inc.

The Church today is brashly confronted with ambiguous teachings and behaviours contrary to the Bible—practices that are being ubiquitously applauded. Michael Scantlebury audaciously sets before us teaching that reveal the "good and bad" of what precisely is meant by *"A little leaven leavens the whole lump."*

If you have entertained unanswered questions of late such as, "Why is there so much hypocrisy in the Church;" "Why is there so much greed in the Church;" "Who is teaching truth and who is teaching in error;" or "Who is sincere versus who is practicing idiocy;" then *Leaven Revealed* delivers sound answers to these valid questions.

Upon reading a few chapters of this book you recognize that Apostle Scantlebury unveils with power and balance... assuring the reader in the end, that the *Leaven of the kingdom of God* we must aspire above all else!

Walter Boston, Jr. – Senior Apostolic Team Leader
C. A. U. S. E. International

I love the idea behind this book. It is fresh, revelatory, and it opens key ideas from the Scripture that have been overlooked for a very long time. With the heart of an apostolic father, Michael Scantlebury unveils the influence of leaven from a Biblical perspective, but also relates it to many of the prevailing problems found in the Church today. Leaven Revealed lays forth a decision for its readers: will I allow my life to be influenced by the leaven of the world and the enemy, or will I allow the Leaven of the Kingdom of God to prevail?

Brad Herman, The Arsenal Bookstore
www.arsenalbooks.com

It is an honor to heartily endorse Apostle Michael Scantlebury's new book. Apostle Michael is a visionary with amazing revelation and Kingdom mindset. Each time I read any of his written work, I am built up and encouraged. The Lord has used him several times to help me see into the situations prophetically.

Trying to understand the Scriptures is like trying to put together a puzzle with the pieces face down unless they are "rightly divided." Apostle Michael helps form the pieces so they all fit together properly and we can see the whole picture clearly. I find this book to be an example of a deep and sincere desire to share a valuable and precious message especially with all who need to hear and understand God's Word. This work is very understandable and shows a depth of comprehension and prayerful interpretation of God's Word.

Dr. Muqaddam Zia – Church Leader, Pakistan
www.prayforpakistan.org

This is a time in our history where The Church is moving to another level of uncovering mysteries and the hidden wisdom of God. We praise God for his anointed servants who through prayer, dedication and commitment of their lives have been staying in His presence long enough to know what God is saying to the Church in these days. Books authored by Dr. Michael Scantlebury are so essential to keep The Church on track and not to allow it to fall victim to spiritual blindness. His latest book "Leaven Revealed" is eye salve to The Church and is a must read for all Pastors, leaders and Believers.

Dr. Michael Scantlebury has been visiting our Church regularly during the past twelve years and has become a dear friend. He is known for his insightful teaching and accurate prophetic word which has been a source of inspiration and encouragement that has kept our Church at Mirihana as a 'going forward' Church despite many obstacles. He brings this same insightful teaching and prophetic gifting through the pages of the book that is before you.

Ajith Abeyratne – Senior Pastor – Mirihana Calvary Church
Chairman, "The Refuge" Home for Abused Children
Board Member of Lanka Bible College
Board Member – Compassion International – Sri Lanka
Former Chairman of Haggai Institute, Sri Lanka and the Chairman of the LEADS Organization
Company Director and former National Coach and Chairman
National Selection Committee of the Sri Lanka Rugby Union

The Book, "Leaven Revealed," is a profound look at the growing effects of "bad leaven" not only as was witnessed in the religious sects of Jesus' Day where the result was false teachings and aberrant practices, but it also delves into the positive upside and the importance of Good Leaven of the Kingdom today, and its influence toward a Strong Foundation, Stability, and the ability to Rightly Divide the Word of Truth and to proclaim Kingdom Advancement!

In a society that is so desensitized to the fleshly dictates of this world certain experiences under the banner of "Charisma and Anointing," have become the foundation of many Believers who build improperly on the latest spiritual fad of the day instead of the Scriptures.

In my estimation, this is the most current and up to date book concerning leaven, a "Must Read," foundational book that must be echoed throughout the Church in order for the Church to be a true Light and Life to the World!

It is with honour and with highest regard to the authorship and publishing thereof that we endorse this book, "Leaven Revealed," as a MASTERPIECE in establishing the Church in present day truth!

Today we need more Apostles, who are Kingdom-Minded Theologians and Exegetes to lay a strong foundation in the Church, and we find this to be true of Apostle Michael Scantlebury!

Dr. Tim Early, for...
Dr. Tim & Theresa Early – Apostles, Founder
The Foundation of the Apostles and Prophets International

Apostle Scantlebury, in this work, has spent time and effort to research and expose the meaning of a rather important concept in Scripture. This treatment clearly enlightens our minds and inspires our hearts. You will find this to be informative and stimulating reading, and adherence to the truths taught, will enable the reader to live a much more productive Christian life. I highly recommend this book.

Apostle Alvin Nicholson
Agape Ministries – Ontario, Canada

TABLE OF CONTENTS

LEAVEN REVEALED

FOREWORD

We are living in a very different world from the one in which I got saved. I was saved in a time when truth was an absolute and there were very few, if any grey areas. Today, we have options; countless types of bread, hundreds of television channels, options on lifestyle and sadly now, many forms of Christianity. Even the Believer is riddled with many options in the Church and these now threaten the absolutes that are the foundation of who we are; absolutes based on Truth as immutable and unchanging.

I believe this book seeks to regain some lost territory in our corporate mind as the Church, the Ekklesia in the principle of what we believe and live. Apostle Scantlebury with a fine toothcomb goes through the Word of God exposing the types of leaven and how they have become a part of the Church in some places of the world today. This work will also be a trumpet call to the unaffected Believer to stay on the wall and watch that this leaven not consume you where you are.

The many challenges to the Truth in the world today are false doctrines, twisted teachings, parallel truths, subjective positions, diluted convictions and quick-sand principles, skewed interpretations all for the 'tickling ear' and comfortable gospel. I do not believe that Jesus Christ intended for His gospel and the Kingdom of God and its message to be comfortable, not that we do not enjoy the power of its demonstration. Yet consistently through the life He lived while He walked the earth, Jesus Christ took and maintained the absolute position. He was a continual challenge to the status quo, questioning authority, as the seat of power shifted from that of the devil to the King of kings.

We need to return to the power of true salvation, where light has no fellowship with darkness; where the true light of the revelation of the Christ dispels areas of darkness. Our mandate is to raise the standard of Jesus Christ without apologising and excusing what we believe. We need to return to the time of absolutes where His Word is the overall authority on matters that concern our world. Like the Apostle Paul and the Apostles of the pre-Nicene period, we need to proclaim our apologetics with a loud clarion voice, falling back on the tried and tested foundation of Apostles and Prophets.

Leaven as an ingredient gives a false sense of growth. True growth is based on fruit that remains, based on the unadulterated power exercised in the hand of God working in the life of a person – nothing falsified, manufactured or duplicated.

This generation of Believer must continue to believe in the immutability of the Word of God, the sanctity of the Covenant of Salvation by the blood of Jesus Christ in His death, burial and resurrection, the power, presence and function of the Holy Spirit, the continual work of sanctification through holiness unto God, the application of truth and faith toward God and the surety of a returning King for a spotless and prepared Bride.

In the face of the levels of corruption in systems of governance and leadership in the world, Jesus Christ remains the only standard of leadership, and thus our only model for emulation as Believers in the Earth.

We are inspired by works such as these that remind us of the necessity of an unquenchable appreciation of who God is and how we are to worship Him, in spirit and in truth. As you read this book, open your heart to the Spirit and Truth of God and let Him work in you for a greater and more exceeding weight of glory.

In this day, Jesus Christ is still preached and remains true now and forever. In this modern day Church, the teachings by Jesus on leaven and those inspired by Him are still as relevant and needed today as if we are physically walking with Christ, physically as did the Twelve. We must take territory and in preparation to celebrate the fullness of every feast and enter into our rest, purge ourselves and the Church of leaven, in its every form, it is time to experience God as He is.

Bishop Tudor Bismark
Jabula Heights
147 Robert Mugabe Road
Harare, Zimbabwe

CHAPTER 1

LEAVEN – BIBLICAL ORIGINS

Leaven or a leavening agent is any one of a number of substances used in dough and batters that causes a foaming action which lightens and softens the finished product. The leavening agent incorporates gas bubbles into the dough through a process of fermentation. Apart from the world of baking, leaven is also introduced figuratively as a substance, element, agent or influence [whether good or bad] that works very subtly to lighten, enliven, corrupt or modify a whole.

In the Scriptures, it is referred to in both good and bad contexts and as such we will be exploring both. In Christian circles it is mostly associated with sin, but a careful study of the word is needed to better understand the complexities of the word.

In case you are not familiar with my previous books[1], I need to reference the "Law of First Mention" which is a concept that is used regularly when studying the Scriptures. It simply means that the very first time any important word is mentioned in the Bible, Scripture gives that word its most complete, and accurate meaning to not only serve as a "*key*" in understanding the word's Biblical concept, but to also provide a foundation for its fuller development in later parts of the Bible. One of the most remarkable evidences of Biblical unity is the *internal* consistency, and no where is this internal consistency more strikingly evident than in this phenomenon which students of the Bible refer to as "*The Law of First Mention*," so let us briefly study this word in its original usage:

---

[1] For more information see the end of this book!

Leaven:
The first time this word was used in Scriptures is found in the Book of Exodus:

"Now the Lord spoke to Moses and Aaron in the land of Egypt, saying, [2]"This month *shall be* your beginning of months; it *shall be* the first month of the year to you. [3]Speak to all the congregation of Israel, saying: 'On the tenth of this month every man shall take for himself a lamb, according to the house of *his* father, a lamb for a household. [4]And if the household is too small for the lamb, let him and his neighbor next to his house take *it* according to the number of the persons; according to each man's need you shall make your count for the lamb. [5]Your lamb shall be without blemish, a male of the first year. You may take *it* from the sheep or from the goats. [6]Now you shall keep it until the fourteenth day of the same month. Then the whole assembly of the congregation of Israel shall kill it at twilight. [7]And they shall take *some* of the blood and put *it* on the two doorposts and on the lintel of the houses where they eat it. [8]Then they shall eat the flesh on that night; roasted in fire, with unleavened bread *and* with bitter *herbs* they shall eat it. [9]Do not eat it raw, nor boiled at all with water, but roasted in fire—its head with its legs and its entrails. [10]You shall let none of it remain until morning, and what remains of it until morning you shall burn with fire. [11]And thus you shall eat it: *with* a belt on your waist, your sandals on your feet, and your staff in your hand. So you shall eat it in haste. It *is* the Lord's Passover. [12]'For I will pass through the land of Egypt on that night, and will strike all the firstborn in the land of Egypt, both man and beast; and against all the gods of Egypt I will execute judgment: I *am* the Lord. [13]Now the blood shall be a sign for you on the houses where you *are*. And when I see the blood, I will pass over you; and the plague shall not be on you to destroy *you* when I strike the land of Egypt. [14]'So this day shall be to you a memorial; and you shall keep it as a feast to the Lord throughout your generations. You shall keep it as a feast by an everlasting ordinance. [15]Seven days you shall eat unleavened bread. On the first day you shall remove leaven from your houses. For whoever eats leavened bread from the first day until the seventh day, that person shall be cut off from Israel. [16]On the first day *there shall be* a holy convocation, and on the seventh day there shall be a holy convocation for you. No manner of work shall be done on them; but *that* which everyone must eat—that only may be prepared by you. [17]So you shall observe *the Feast of* Unleavened Bread, for on this same day I will have brought your armies out of the land of Egypt. Therefore you shall observe this day throughout your generations as an everlasting ordinance. [18]In the first *month,* on the fourteenth day of the month at evening, you shall eat unleavened bread, until the twenty-first day of the month at evening. [19]For seven days no leaven shall be found in your houses, since whoever eats what is leavened, that same person shall be cut off from the congregation of Israel, whether *he is* a stranger or a native of the land. [20]You shall eat nothing leavened; in all your dwellings you shall eat unleavened bread.'" [21]Then Moses called for all the elders of Israel and said to them, "Pick out and take lambs for yourselves according to your families, and kill the Passover *lamb.* [22]And you shall take a bunch of hyssop, dip *it* in the blood that *is* in the basin, and strike the lintel and the two doorposts with the blood that *is* in the basin. And none of you shall go out of the door of his house until morning. [23]For the Lord will pass through to strike the Egyptians; and when He sees the blood on the lintel and on the two doorposts, the Lord will pass over the door and not allow the destroyer to come into your houses to strike *you.* [24]And you shall observe this thing as an ordinance for you and your sons forever. [25]It will come to pass when you come to the land, which the Lord will give you, just as He promised, that you shall keep this service. [26]And it shall be, when your children say to you, 'What do you mean by this service?' [27]that you shall say, 'It *is* the Passover sacrifice of the Lord, who passed over the houses of the children of Israel in Egypt when He struck the Egyptians and delivered our households.'" So the people bowed their heads and worshiped. [28]Then the children of Israel went away and did *so;* just as the Lord had commanded Moses and Aaron, so they did." Exodus 12:1-28

After 450 years of slavery in the land of Egypt, the Children of Israel were about to be released by the Word of the Lord! The way the Lord was going to release them was very significant and would do well for us to spend a little time in exploring this.

Israel was a nation that was formed while under bondage in the Land of Egypt. While under the hard task masters of Egypt the Children of Israel cried out to God Who heard their cry and decided to liberate them. Through the liberation process, He established the Passover [which required that a Lamb was sacrificed for each household] to serve the nation of Israel and their spiritual needs, but He also established it to be a shadow of what was to come with Jesus' death, burial and resurrection. This was accomplished by the slaying of a lamb.

The Passover included the following principles:

- The Lamb must be without spot or blemish.
- The Lamb must be killed at twilight.
- The Blood of the Lamb was to be placed on the doorposts and the lintels of every house.
- The Flesh of the Lamb was to be eaten.
- The Lamb was to be eaten with Bread – *without any leaven.*
- An Ordinance was established to last forever.
- It was to be known as The Passover.

A Lamb For Each Household:
This ordinance is so filled with prophetic significance. God from the very onset was establishing a powerful truth.

In the study of Scripture Egypt is referred to as a type of the world. The Lamb is also known as a type of Jesus Christ [The Perfect Lamb of God]. When Jesus Christ came to earth one of His functions was to take away the sins of the world, as the Lamb of God. Here is what John the Baptist, His forerunner proclaimed:

> "The next day John saw Jesus coming toward him and said, "Look, the Lamb of God, who takes away the sin of the world! [30]This is the one I meant when I said, 'A man who comes after me has surpassed me because he was before me.' [31]I myself did not know him, but the reason I came baptizing with water was that he might be revealed to Israel." [32]Then John gave this testimony: "I saw the Spirit come down from heaven as a dove and remain on him. [33]I would not have known him, except that the one who sent me to baptize with water told me, 'The man on whom you see the Spirit come down and remain is he who will baptize with the Holy Spirit.' [34]I have seen and I testify that this is the Son of God." John 1:29-34

Just as it was back then for Israel to be redeemed from Egypt [a type of the world] and become the people of God [a type of the Church/Believer], a spotless lamb had to be slain for each home. Even today the only way that one can be saved from the destroying angel of death [spiritual death] is to apply the Blood of the slain lamb. The Blood of the Lamb [Jesus Christ] must be applied to our lives.

The Lamb Had To Be Spotless Or 'Without Blemish':
We also know that this was true of Jesus Christ the Perfect Lamb of God sent to take away the sins of the world. Apostle Peter attests to this:

> "For you know that it was not with perishable things such as silver or gold that you were redeemed from the empty way of life handed down to you from your forefathers, [19]but with the precious blood of Christ, a lamb without blemish or defect. [20]He was chosen before the creation of the world, but was revealed in these last times for your sake." 1 Peter 1:18-20

And in Paul's letter to the Corinthian church:
> "God made him who had no sin to be sin for us, so that in him we might become the righteousness of God." 2 Corinthians 5:21

The Lamb Had To Be Killed At Twilight:
From all historical records including the Bible, Jesus Christ the Perfect Lamb of God was crucified at around 9:00 AM Jewish time. Because this was nowhere near twilight, even meteorological phenomena shifted for a period of three hours. In that time, the entire region suddenly become dark in order for twilight to be upon the earth when Jesus Christ, The Perfect Lamb of God bled and died on the Cross. The following is Mark's account of that event:

> "Let this Christ, this King of Israel, come down now from the cross, that we may see and believe." Those crucified with him also heaped insults on him. [33]At the sixth hour darkness came over the whole land until the ninth hour. [34]And at the ninth hour Jesus cried out in a loud voice, "Eloi, Eloi, lama sabachthani?"—which means, "My God, my God, why have you forsaken me?" [35]When some of those standing near heard this, they said, "Listen, he's calling Elijah." [36]One man ran, filled a sponge with wine vinegar, put it on a stick, and offered it to Jesus to drink. "Now leave him alone. Let's see if Elijah comes to take him down," he said. [37]With a loud cry, Jesus breathed his last." Mark 15:32-37

The Blood Of The Lamb Was To Be Placed On The Doorposts And The Lintels Of Every House:

Although Jesus Christ, the Lamb of God was slain for the entire world, unless His blood is applied to one's life or as a family there will be no salvation! When the angel of death passes, without salvation there is just no hope. The blood had to be applied to the doorposts and the lintels for the angel to pass over! Every true Born-Again Believer in Jesus Christ, who is a part of His Church *must* be Born-Again through the finished work of Calvary – through the shed Blood of Jesus Christ being applied to one's life!

The Flesh Of The Lamb Was To Be Eaten:

Jesus Christ Himself as the Perfect Lamb of God made that very assertion of fact, when He said to His disciples as recorded in:

> "Then the Jews began to argue sharply among themselves, "How can this man give us his flesh to eat?" [53]Jesus said to them, "I tell you the truth, unless you eat the flesh of the Son of Man and drink his blood, you have no life in you. [54]Whoever eats my flesh and drinks my blood has eternal life, and I will raise him up at the last day. [55]For my flesh is real food and my blood is real drink. [56]Whoever eats my flesh and drinks my blood remains in me, and I in him. [57]Just as the living Father sent me and I live because of the Father, so the one who feeds on me will live because of me." John 6:52-57

Every time we partake of Holy Communion we are reminded of the fact that the Perfect Lamb of God without spot or blemish, Who knew no sin died for us on the Cross and that He rose again in order that we might have eternal life! We are reminded of the fact that we are partakers of the Lamb that was slain!

The Lamb Was To Be Eaten With Bread – Without Any Leaven:

The night before Jesus Christ went to the Cross, He met with his disciples in the upper room where He took Unleavened Bread and broke it and gave them to eat, telling them that it was His Body! Here is how the Apostle Luke records it:

> "Then came the day of Unleavened Bread on which the Passover lamb had to be sacrificed. [8]Jesus sent Peter and John, saying, "Go and make preparations for us to eat the Passover." [9]"Where do you want us to prepare for it?" they asked. [10]He replied, "As you enter the city, a man carrying a jar of water will meet you. Follow him to the house that he enters, [11]and say to the owner of the house, 'The Teacher asks: Where is the guest room, where I may eat the Passover with my disciples?' [12]He will show you a large upper room, all furnished. Make preparations there." [13]They left and found things just as Jesus had told them.

So they prepared the Passover. [14]When the hour came, Jesus and his apostles reclined at the table. [15]And he said to them, "I have eagerly desired to eat this Passover with you before I suffer. [16]For I tell you, I will not eat it again until it finds fulfillment in the kingdom of God." [17]After taking the cup, he gave thanks and said, "Take this and divide it among you. [18]For I tell you I will not drink again of the fruit of the vine until the kingdom of God comes." [19]And he took bread, gave thanks and broke it, and gave it to them, saying, "This is my body given for you; do this in remembrance of me." [20]In the same way, after the supper he took the cup, saying, "This cup is the new covenant in my blood, which is poured out for you." Luke 22:7-20

At that point Jesus Christ was transforming the annual Jewish Feast of Passover from an Old Testament ritual with the natural blood and body of a lamb to a New Covenant reality, with spiritual significance to the Perfect Lamb of God, Jesus Christ!

I like what the Apostle Paul had to say concerning this:

"In the following directives I have no praise for you, for your meetings do more harm than good. [18]In the first place, I hear that when you come together as a church, there are divisions among you, and to some extent I believe it. [19]No doubt there have to be differences among you to show which of you have God's approval. [20]When you come together, it is not the Lord's Supper you eat, [21]for as you eat, each of you goes ahead without waiting for anybody else. One remains hungry, another gets drunk. [22]Don't you have homes to eat and drink in? Or do you despise the church of God and humiliate those who have nothing? What shall I say to you? Shall I praise you for this? Certainly not! [23]For I received from the Lord what I also passed on to you: The Lord Jesus, on the night He was betrayed, took bread, [24]and when he had given thanks, he broke it and said, "This is my body, which is for you; do this in remembrance of me." [25]In the same way, after supper he took the cup, saying, "This cup is the new covenant in my blood; do this, whenever you drink it, in remembrance of me." [26]For whenever you eat this bread and drink this cup, you proclaim the Lord's death until he comes. [27]Therefore, whoever eats the bread or drinks the cup of the Lord in an unworthy manner will be guilty of sinning against the body and blood of the Lord. [28]A man ought to examine himself before he eats of the bread and drinks of the cup. [29]For anyone who eats and drinks without recognizing the body of the Lord eats and drinks judgment on himself. [30]That is why many among you are weak and sick, and a number of you have fallen asleep. [31]But if we judged ourselves, we would not come under judgment. [32]When we are judged by the Lord, we are being disciplined so that we will not be condemned with the world. [33]So then, my brothers, when you come together to eat, wait for each other. [34]If anyone is hungry, he should eat at home, so that when you meet together it may not result in judgment. And when I come I will give further directions." 1 Corinthians 11:17-34

CHAPTER 2

AN UNDERSTANDING OF THE FEASTS

I n order to establish the relevance of leaven and what it means to the Believer, we need to briefly explore the Feasts that were celebrated by the Children of Israel and how they relate to us as Born-Again Believers in Jesus Christ. It may seem laborious at the outset, but the revisiting of these portions of Scripture is very necessary as we shall see.

There were three major annual feasts in Israel and the Passover was the first to be celebrated. All these feasts have tremendous Spiritual significance for the New Testament Believer. Let me give you a breakdown of these feasts:

The Feast of the Passover, also known as the Feast of Unleavened Bread was further subdivided into three components:

Passover began at twilight on the fourteenth day of the first month according to Leviticus 23:4-5

"These are the LORD's appointed feasts, the sacred assemblies you are to proclaim at their appointed times: ⁵The LORD's Passover begins at twilight on the fourteenth day of the first month."

More specifics are found in the following passage:
"The LORD said to Moses and Aaron in Egypt, ²"This month is to be for you the first month, the first month of your year. ³Tell the whole community of Israel that on the tenth day of this month each man is to take a lamb for his family, one for each household. ⁴If any household is too

small for a whole lamb, they must share one with their nearest neighbour, having taken into account the number of people there are. You are to determine the amount of lamb needed in accordance with what each person will eat. [5]The animals you choose must be year-old males without defect, and you may take them from the sheep or the goats. [6]Take care of them until the fourteenth day of the month, when all the people of the community of Israel must slaughter them at twilight. [7]Then they are to take some of the blood and put it on the sides and tops of the doorframes of the houses where they eat the lambs. [8]That same night they are to eat the meat roasted over the fire, along with bitter herbs, and bread made without yeast. [9]Do not eat the meat raw or cooked in water, but roast it over the fire—head, legs and inner parts. [10]Do not leave any of it till morning; if some is left till morning, you must burn it. [11]This is how you are to eat it: with your cloak tucked into your belt, your sandals on your feet and your staff in your hand. Eat it in haste; it is the LORD's Passover. [12]"On that same night I will pass through Egypt and strike down every firstborn— both men and animals—and I will bring judgment on all the gods of Egypt. I am the LORD. [13]The blood will be a sign for you on the houses where you are; and when I see the blood, I will pass over you. No destructive plague will touch you when I strike Egypt. [14]"This is a day you are to commemorate; for the generations to come you shall celebrate it as a festival to the LORD -a lasting ordinance. [15]For seven days you are to eat bread made without yeast. On the first day remove the yeast from your houses, for whoever eats anything with yeast in it from the first day through the seventh must be cut off from Israel. [16]On the first day hold a sacred assembly, and another one on the seventh day. Do no work at all on these days, except to prepare food for everyone to eat—that is all you may do. [17]"Celebrate the Feast of Unleavened Bread, because it was on this very day that I brought your divisions out of Egypt. Celebrate this day as a lasting ordinance for the generations to come. [18]In the first month you are to eat bread made without yeast, from the evening of the fourteenth day until the evening of the twenty-first day. [19]For seven days no yeast is to be found in your houses. And whoever eats anything with yeast in it must be cut off from the community of Israel, whether he is an alien or native-born. [20]Eat nothing made with yeast. Wherever you live, you must eat unleavened bread." [21]Then Moses summoned all the elders of Israel and said to them, "Go at once and select the animals for your families and slaughter the Passover lamb. [22]Take a bunch of hyssop, dip it into the blood in the basin and put some of the blood on the top and on both sides of the doorframe. Not one of you shall go out the door of his house until morning. [23]When the LORD goes through the land to strike down the Egyptians, he will see the blood on the top and sides of the doorframe and will pass over that doorway, and he will not permit the destroyer to enter your houses and strike you down." Exodus 12:1-23

"Observe the month of Abib and celebrate the Passover of the LORD your God, because in the month of Abib he brought you out of Egypt by night. [2]Sacrifice as the Passover to the LORD your God an animal from your flock or herd at the place the LORD will choose as a dwelling for his Name. [3]Do not eat it with bread made with yeast, but for seven days eat unleavened bread, the bread of affliction, because you left Egypt in haste—so that all the days of your life you may remember the time of your departure from Egypt." Deuteronomy 16:1-3

Jesus Christ is our Passover:

"Get rid of the old yeast [leaven] that you may be a new batch without yeast [leaven]—as you really are. For Christ, our Passover lamb, has been sacrificed." [NKJV Parenthesis added] 1 Corinthians 5:7

The second component of the Passover – The Unleavened Bread:

"In the first month you are to eat bread made without yeast, from the evening of the fourteenth day until the evening of the twenty-first day." Exodus 12:18

"Celebrate the Feast of Unleavened Bread; for seven days eat bread made without yeast, as I commanded you. Do this at the appointed time in the month of Abib, for in that month you came out of Egypt. "No one is to appear before me empty-handed." Exodus 23:15

"On the fifteenth day of that month the LORD's Feast of Unleavened Bread begins; for seven days you must eat bread made without yeast. [7]On the first day hold a sacred assembly and do no regular work. [8]For seven days present an offering made to the LORD by fire. And on the seventh day hold a sacred assembly and do no regular work." Leviticus 23:6-8

"Do not eat it with bread made with yeast, but for seven days eat unleavened bread, the bread of affliction, because you left Egypt in haste—so that all the days of your life you may remember the time of your departure from Egypt. [4]Let no yeast be found in your possession in all your land for seven days. Do not let any of the meat you sacrifice on the evening of the first day remain until morning." Deuteronomy 16:3-4

Jesus Christ is our Unleavened Bread:

"On the first day of the Feast of Unleavened Bread, the disciples came to Jesus and asked, "Where do you want us to make preparations for you to eat the Passover?"... [26]While they were eating, Jesus took bread, gave thanks and broke it, and gave it to his disciples, saying, "Take and eat; this is my body." [27]Then he took the cup, gave thanks and offered it to them, saying, "Drink from it, all of you. [28]This is my blood of the covenant, which is poured out for many for the forgiveness of sins." Matthew 26:17, 26-28

"For I received from the Lord what I also passed on to you:

The Lord Jesus, on the night he was betrayed, took bread, [24]and when he had given thanks, he broke it and said, "This is my body, which is for you; do this in remembrance of me." [25]In the same way, after supper he took the cup, saying, "This cup is the new covenant in my blood; do this, whenever you drink it, in remembrance of me." [26]For whenever you eat this bread and drink this cup, you proclaim the Lord's death until he comes." 1 Corinthians 11:23-26

The Third Component of the Passover – The Sheaf of First-fruits:
"Speak to the Israelites and say to them: 'When you enter the land I am going to give you and you reap its harvest, bring to the priest a sheaf of the first grain you harvest. [11]He is to wave the sheaf before the LORD so it will be accepted on your behalf; the priest is to wave it on the day after the Sabbath. [12]On the day you wave the sheaf, you must sacrifice as a burnt offering to the LORD a lamb a year old without defect, [13]together with its grain offering of two-tenths of an ephah of fine flour mixed with oil—an offering made to the LORD by fire, a pleasing aroma—and its drink offering of a quarter of a hin of wine. [14]You must not eat any bread, or roasted or new grain, until the very day you bring this offering to your God. This is to be a lasting ordinance for the generations to come, wherever you live." Leviticus 23:10-14

All these Feasts of the Old Testament were fulfilled in Jesus Christ Who became the Perfect Lamb that was slain. His Blood was applied to our lives as Believers thus saving us from eternal death!

Jesus Christ is our Sheaf of First-fruits:
"But Christ has indeed been raised from the dead, the first-fruits of those who have fallen asleep. [21]For since death came through a man, the resurrection of the dead comes also through a man. [22]For as in Adam all die, so in Christ all will be made alive. [23]But each in his own turn: Christ, the first-fruits; then, when he comes, those who belong to him." 1 Corinthians 15:20-23

From this we have seen that the very first Feast that was instituted by God to be an everlasting ordinance was the Feast of Passover. On the 15th day of this feast of Passover, there was the institution of the Unleavened Bread which represents Sanctification for the Believer by taking leaven [sin or anything that defiles us] from our lives and homes! The Israelites who continued to use leaven were to be cut off from the tribe of Israel. We know from experience that the Born-Again experience affords us Salvation and the means to live a sanctified, holy life!

The Bible has a lot more to say about *leaven*. In the New Testament there are at least six types of *leaven* spoken about and we will do well to explore them in detail, in order to ensure that our lives are completely free of the first five, and completely influenced by the sixth!

These types of leaven include the following:

1. The leaven of the Pharisees
2. The leaven of the Sadducees
3. The leaven of the Galatians
4. The leaven of Herod
5. The leaven of the Corinthians
6. The Leaven of the Kingdom of God

CHAPTER 3

SPIRITUAL SIGNIFICANCE OF LEAVEN

Various substances are known to have fermenting qualities. There weren't any active dry granules of yeast in those days, hence the making of bread with ordinary leaven consisted of a lump of active *dough* in a high state of fermentation which was mixed into the mass of dough prepared for baking. This had to be ongoing in order to keep the supply of leaven on hand and active. No leaven meant no bread, so it was favourable to have it on hand to bake the day's bread supply. It was absolutely necessary to hold back a small amount to propagate the next batch of bread.

The interesting thing is that the use of leaven was strictly forbidden in all offerings made to the Lord by fire. During the Passover, the Jews were commanded to put out every particle of leaven from their houses. This was to be done according to the letter of the Law. This necessity of purging every bit of leaven from their lives as a sacrifice unto the Lord sets a precedent for the rich comparisons drawn for us as New Testament Believers.

The Spiritual Significance of Leaven in The New Testament:
The Apostle Paul writing by the power of the Holy Spirit to the Galatians and Corinthian churches had to address rampant sexual impurity and the stronghold of the practices of Judaism; and bondage to the Law in each of these founding churches respectively, puts it succinctly:

"Your glorying is not good. Do you not know that a little leaven leavens the whole lump? [7]Therefore purge out the old leaven, that you may be a new lump, since you truly are unleavened. For indeed Christ, our Passover, was sacrificed for us. [8]Therefore let us keep the feast, not with old leaven, nor with the leaven of malice and wickedness, but with the unleavened bread of sincerity and truth." 1 Corinthians 5:6-8

"Stand fast therefore in the liberty by which Christ has made us free, and do not be entangled again with a yoke of bondage. [2]Indeed I, Paul, say to you that if you become circumcised, Christ will profit you nothing. [3]And I testify again to every man who becomes circumcised that he is a debtor to keep the whole law. [4]You have become estranged from Christ, you who attempt to be justified by law; you have fallen from grace. [5]For we through the Spirit eagerly wait for the hope of righteousness by faith. [6]For in Christ Jesus neither circumcision nor uncircumcision avails anything, but faith working through love. [7]You ran well. Who hindered you from obeying the truth? [8]This persuasion does not come from Him who calls you. [9]A little leaven leavens the whole lump." Galatians 5:1-9

How Do We as Believers Remain Free Of Leaven?

We need to go back to the origins of this command with the principle called the Law of First Mention and see what happened where the principle is first mentioned in the Bible and how it carries the same meaning throughout the rest of the Bible.

- The Passover was established as a symbol of the Lord sparing us from death because of the Blood of the Lamb [Jesus Christ] that was applied on the doorposts of our lives.

- The children of Israel also left Egypt [a type of the world] in haste so they did not have time for their bread [lives] to become leavened – Exodus 12:39. Had they lingered in Egypt they would have had ample opportunity to have their bread leavened.

- So it is with us as long as we keep pressing on in the things of God and keep ourselves from the corrupting influences of the world, the flesh and the devil – we will be free of leaven [sin and corruption].

I tell you if we begin to lose sight of what the Lord has called us to, or if we begin to lose sight of the Lord's Glory and the nature of Jesus Christ, before long we will become filled with the leaven of malice and wickedness.

- Do you realize that there is only one way to keep a stream of water clean and pure? – That is to keep it flowing!

- The Bible declares this in 1 Corinthians 8:1-3 – "Now concerning things offered to idols: We know that we all have knowledge. Knowledge puffs up, but love edifies. ²And if anyone thinks that he knows anything, he knows nothing yet as he ought to know. ³But if anyone loves God, this one is known by Him." A lot of times leaven seeps into our lives when we think that we have arrived because of some new revelation or some knowledge of the Word of God. We all of a sudden think that we are like God and we are better than everyone else – causing leaven to step into our lives. It is the very same temptation Eve and Adam found themselves in and were cast out of the Garden of God. This is why *Revelation Must Be Progressive – Truth Is Progressive – We Can Never Arrive Until We Are In Our New Bodies From Heaven*!

Now that we know how to remain free of *leaven*, in the next chapter, we will look at the different types of *leaven* that we need to stay away from.

CHAPTER 4

THE LEAVEN OF THE PHARISEES

Although leaven is a necessity of life for bakers and for those who enjoy their baked products, the most prominent idea associated with leaven in connection with the Bible is the idea of *corruption*. As we stated earlier, dough becomes bread due to fermentation, where carbon dioxide [poisonous gas in its purest form] has infiltrated the bread mass to turn it into a souring heap. The smell of bread fresh from the oven causes salivation at the outset, and the warm bread dripping with butter is a welcome taste sensation to the most discriminating palate. But prior to that reality, the bread becomes a rotten, corrupted mass if you will, in the process of fermentation. It is to this rotten property of leaven that our Saviour points to when He speaks of the "leaven [that is, the corrupt doctrine] of the Pharisees."

"Then Jesus said to them, "Take heed and beware of the leaven of the Pharisees and the Sadducees." [7]And they reasoned among themselves, saying, "It is because we have taken no bread." [8]But Jesus, being aware of it, said to them, "O you of little faith, why do you reason among yourselves because you have brought no bread? [9]Do you not yet understand, or remember the five loaves of the five thousand and how many baskets you took up? [10]Nor the seven loaves of the four thousand and how many large baskets you took up? [11]How is it you do not understand that I did not speak to you concerning bread?– but to beware of the leaven of the Pharisees and Sadducees." [12]Then they understood that He did not tell them to beware of the leaven of bread, but of the doctrine of the Pharisees and Sadducees." Matthew 16:6-12

The Pharisees – Who They Were:
They were a religious sect revered by the Jews for their religious standing. They were quick to judge, quick to condemn and quick to quell every new wave of apparent religion lest they be dethroned from their positions of power. Although they no longer exist in terms of a sect, if we study who the Pharisees were and what they believed and practiced we would be shocked to find they are still among us today.

You see, a spirit residing within a sect can be passed on and although the sect died out, many people are bewitched by their teachings and practices, not just in Judaism but also in Christian circles. If you have been in contact with this pharisaical spirit, you might not even know or recognize it as such but they will correct you according to what they believe without any mind of what the Scriptures actually say. They will not necessarily be in relationship with you but will lord their opinion over you that they are indeed the voice of God, or at least His special messenger.

The Pharisees tried to correct Jesus Christ by using their own made up laws. They made up their own laws that were not from God to correct Jesus Christ. Much of Jesus Christ's earthly ministry was in conflict with their teachings, and more often than not He was addressing the religion of the Pharisees that they perpetrated upon the people. Due to their religious appearance and apparent piety, they managed to use this absolute power to brainwash the masses with their lofty ideas without any confirmation in Scripture. The Pharisees wanted everyone to learn and follow their ways and interpretations of the Scripture. By having a strong following, they strengthened their hold on the people: the stronger they became, the more corruption they could spread.

Jesus Christ clearly showed us how the Pharisees needed to be handled. He did not bow, nor submit to man made laws, traditions of men or false Bible interpretations by famous, well-known religious men. We have that charge as Believers to not bow to the wiles of men, but to uphold and measure things by the same authority and standard used by Jesus Christ – The Word of God.

The Pharisees were not psychic and no other human can force you to submit to their words unless you want to do so. However, these modern day Pharisee types have clever ways to convince you by using guilt, fear and outright spiritual manipulation just like the Pharisees.

Is this not what we see taking place today? Many want the people in the Church to submit to the word they are prepared to give under the guise of the anointing, but it is often a word that is unfounded and not in line with the Bible. Paul admonishes us in 1 Corinthians 4:6: "Now, brothers, I have applied these things to myself and Apollos for your benefit, so that you may learn from us the meaning of the saying, "Do not go beyond [exceed] what is written." Then you will not take pride in one man over against another."

Apostle Paul gave this admonition so that pride would not have an opportunity to operate and puff someone up. The Pharisees added to the interpretation of the Scriptures. They became superior in their own minds and had people convinced that they heard from God. It happens time and time again when someone leads well-meaning students of the Word beyond the Scriptures instead of correctly explaining what is contained in them. The person committing such folly is being spiritually destructive to himself and to others who listen to him. This is no small matter to be glossed over. In time, the Pharisees brought almost the whole nation of Israel into their bondage by obedience to their non-biblical teachings.

Intentional false teaching has its source in pride. This is why Jesus Christ warned of the "leaven of the Pharisees", contained in both their teachings and practices. Their own arrogance and pride had them reject Jesus Christ's words. When the Pharisees disputed with Jesus Christ over His claims, He pointed them to the Word. For example:

"So the Pharisees and teachers of the law asked Jesus, "Why don't your disciples live according to the tradition of the elders instead of eating their food with 'unclean' hands?" [6]He replied, "Isaiah was right when he prophesied about you hypocrites; as it is written: " 'These people honour me with their lips, but their hearts are far from me. [7]They worship me in vain; their teachings are but rules taught by men.' [8]You have let go of the commands of God and are holding on to the traditions of men." [9]And he said to them: "You have a fine way of setting aside the commands of God in order to observe your own traditions!" Mark 7:5-9

The Leaven Of The Pharisees:

[2]Leaven of the Pharisees"—it's a curious phrase. Why did Jesus Christ feel compelled to warn His disciples to avoid it? Would you recognize this "state of leavening" if you saw it today? The answer to these questions is important, not just for the Passover season, but throughout the year.

What is this "leaven of the Pharisees"? You will find a direct answer in Luke 12:1. But first we need to consider Luke Chapter 11 in order to understand Jesus Christ's answer. He prefaced His analogy of the leaven of the Pharisees by the following six woes:

"When Jesus had finished speaking, a Pharisee invited him to eat with him; so he went in and reclined at the table. [38]But the Pharisee, noticing that Jesus did not first wash before the meal, was surprised. [39]Then the Lord said to him, "Now then, you Pharisees clean the outside of the cup and dish, but inside you are full of greed and wickedness. [40]You foolish people! Did not the one who made the outside make the inside also? [41]But give what is inside the dish to the poor, and everything will be clean for you. [42]"*Woe to you Pharisees*, because you give God a tenth of your mint, rue and all other kinds of garden herbs, but you neglect justice and the love of God. You should have practiced the latter without leaving the former undone. [43]"*Woe to you Pharisees*, because you love the most important seats in the synagogues and greetings in the marketplaces. [44]"*Woe to you*, because you are like unmarked graves, which men walk over without knowing it."

---

[2] "Beware of the Leaven of the Pharisees" by Robert Dick – United Church of God: www.ucg.org/un/un0203

^{45}One of the experts in the law answered him, "Teacher, when you say these things, you insult us also." ^{46}Jesus replied, "And you experts in the law, *woe to you*, because you load people down with burdens they can hardly carry, and you yourselves will not lift one finger to help them. ^{47}"*Woe to you*, because you build tombs for the prophets, and it was your forefathers who killed them. ^{48}So you testify that you approve of what your forefathers did; they killed the prophets, and you build their tombs. ^{49}Because of this, God in his wisdom said, 'I will send them prophets and apostles, some of whom they will kill and others they will persecute.' ^{50}Therefore this generation will be held responsible for the blood of all the prophets that has been shed since the beginning of the world, ^{51}from the blood of Abel to the blood of Zechariah, who was killed between the altar and the sanctuary. Yes, I tell you, this generation will be held responsible for it all. ^{52}"*Woe to you* experts in the law, because you have taken away the key to knowledge. You yourselves have not entered, and you have hindered those who were entering." ^{53}When Jesus left there, the Pharisees and the teachers of the law began to oppose him fiercely and to besiege him with questions, ^{54}waiting to catch him in something he might say." [Italics added] Luke 11:37-54

And finally Jesus Christ sums it up in the following: "In the meantime, when an innumerable multitude had gathered together, so that they trampled one another, He began to say to His disciples first of all, 'Beware of *the leaven of the Pharisees, which is hypocrisy.*'" [Italics added]. And Jesus Christ's astute observation regarding this hypocrisy was just the tip of the iceberg and the problem. There was a much deeper root which had to be uncovered.

Hypocrisy Defined:
"Hypocrisy" occurs only once in the Old Testament as the translation of choneph [Isaiah 32:6, the Revised Version (British and American) "profaneness"]; chaneph, from which it is derived, means properly "to cover," "to hide," or "becloud," hence, to pollute, to be

polluted or defiled, to make profane, to seduce; as a substantive it is translated "hypocrite"

"Hypocrite" comes from the Greek word "hupokrites" and refers to someone who is acting or pretending. It was the custom of Greek and Roman stage actors to speak in large masks with mechanical devices for augmenting the force of the voice. These actors would conceal their real faces and change their real voices and were called hupokrites, or hypocrites.

It also comes from the Greek word "hupokrisis" and is rendered – acting under a feigned part, i.e. [figuratively] deceit ["hypocrisy"]: also "a reply, an answer" "play-acting," as the actors spoke in dialogue; hence, "pretence, hypocrisy"; it is translated "hypocrisy" – *pretending to act from one motive, whereas another motive really inspires the act.*

Jesus Christ likened the conduct of the Pharisees to actors – men pretending or playing a role. The Pharisees of Jesus Christ's day were a powerful leadership body who claimed to be more zealous and more righteous than the rest of Jewish society. They set themselves up as models of what was right and godly, yet in Jesus Christ's eyes their example was actually destructive. In Jesus Christ's estimation the conduct of these men had a corrupting effect upon those who followed their example – a leavening effect, if you will.

It is interesting that early on Jesus Christ forcefully addressed the issue of hypocrisy in the Sermon on the Mount. You might call Matthew 6:1-18 – a primer on identifying hypocrisy. The hypocrites give offerings for the purpose of being seen and admired [verses 1-2]; they pray to impress men with their voices and their words [verse 5]; and they do all they can to look miserable when they fast so they will be admired for their sacrifice and pitied for their discomfort [verse 16]. Jesus Christ's message to His disciples was simply, "If you do it this way, men's admiration will be your total reward since I will not be looking or listening."

Most people who profess to be Christians get this elementary point. How often do you see someone stand up and brag about how much they give, or blow a trumpet to announce their offering or look so tousled, unshaven and unkempt that you have to ask, "Are you fasting today?" This is just the beginning of it all as the leavening effect of hypocrisy is far broader.

Hypocrisy and Malicious Intent:
Most of us are familiar with the passage in Matthew 22:15-18 where the Pharisees brought a coin to Jesus Christ bearing Caesar's image. They asked Him if it was appropriate to pay taxes. The Jews of Jesus Christ's time hated the Roman occupation, but this was the perfectly devised question to trap Jesus Christ. If He was to say "yes, paying taxes was okay," the Jews would be alienated and slighted. If Jesus said." no, you should not pay taxes," it would be considered treasonous and could open Him up to prosecution by the Roman government. Jesus Christ being omniscient recognized their trap and refuted them at their own game when in verse 18, he says to them... "Why do you test Me, you hypocrites?" In this instance, hypocrisy was the masking of their malicious intent. Jesus did not mince any words.

Verses 15 through 18 make it clear that their intent towards Jesus Christ was malicious. "Then the Pharisees went and plotted how they might entangle Him in His talk. And they sent to Him their disciples with the Herodians, saying "Teacher, we know that You are true and teach the way of God in truth; nor do You care about anyone, for You do not regard the person of men. Tell us therefore what do You think?" Here is a clear example of malicious intent. With smiling faces and flattering words they spoke to him from a theological standpoint, all the while seeking to injure Jesus Christ by baiting a trap for Him.

Apostle Paul, who had been a Pharisee before his conversion, could easily see the connection between leaven and malicious intent. In his letter to the Corinthians, written at the Passover season, Apostle Paul exhorted, "Therefore let us keep the feast, not with old leaven, nor with the leaven of malice and wickedness, but with the unleavened bread of sincerity and truth" [1 Corinthians 5:8]. This is not where the extent of the leaven of the Pharisees ends in Scripture.

A Second Form of Leaven:
In Matthew Chapter 16, Scripture shows that the leaven of the
Pharisees goes beyond hypocrisy. Following the miracle of the
fishes and loaves, the Pharisees confronted Jesus Christ as they
sought a sign. He called them hypocrites to their faces and
offered no sign but the sign of Jonah, who after much chaos
obeyed the call of God to preach repentance to Nineveh. Later
He warned His disciples, "'Take heed and beware of the leaven
of the Pharisees and the Sadducees" [Matthew 16:6]. The
disciples did not at first understand what He meant. Jesus Christ
called the Pharisees hypocrites in verse 3, but the disciples didn't
automatically make a connection.

It is quite likely the disciples were initially blinded by a guilty
conscience. They thought they had received a subtle scolding
because no one remembered to purchase food for the group
[Matthew 16:7]. Jesus Christ explained that He wasn't dependent
upon whether they remembered to buy groceries! After all, hadn't
He just fed a huge multitude with seven loaves and a few fish?
With their guilty consciences relieved, they hit upon His true
intent which is described in verse 12, "Then they understood that
He did not tell them to beware of the leaven of bread, but of the
doctrine of the Pharisees and Sadducees."

The leaven of the Pharisees is more than hypocrisy; it is also their
false doctrine. But how or why is their doctrine equated to leaven
of the corrupt kind? We will find as we go along that there is an
inextricable link between the hypocrisy of the Pharisees and the
doctrines of the Pharisees.

Doctrine and Hypocrisy:
The clearest connection between the hypocrisy of the Pharisees
and their doctrine is seen in Mark 7:1-9, where the Pharisees
complained about the disciples eating with unwashed hands. It
should be understood that the traditions, or rulings, passed down
from generation to generation by the wise men of the pharisaical
persuasion took on the power of law. To the mind of a Pharisee
the sayings of their elders were as binding as the Scriptures. In
fact, Jesus Christ implies they were even seen as more binding than

the Law of God if the two came into conflict. To Jesus Christ this was hypocritical. How can a body of men who claim to be the most righteous observers of the Law of God create traditions that nullify the Law of God and still claim righteousness? This didn't make sense. Due to this incongruence, Jesus Christ saw their doctrines as hypocritical.

As we continue in Mark Chapter 7, we can see the conflict. The Pharisees came to Jesus Christ and challenged Him by saying, "Why do Your disciples not walk according to the traditions of the elders, but eat bread with unwashed hands?" [Mark 7:5]. Jesus Christ responded, "Well did Isaiah prophesy of you hypocrites, as it is written: 'This people honours Me with their lips, but their heart is far from Me, and in vain they worship Me teaching as doctrines the commandments of men.'" [Mark 7:6-7].

Jesus Christ continued His rebuke in Mark 7:8-13, giving examples of traditions passed down by the elders that directly contravened the Law of God. His final summation was that in so many areas of their lives, they had put aside the Law of God in preference to their traditions which exalted them as "perfect leaders." To Jesus Christ this was hypocritical of a body that claimed superior righteousness since the Laws of God are righteousness [Psalm 119:172].

For further examples where this word hypocrisy is used, you can read the following passages from the Scriptures: Matthew Chapter 23; Mark 12:15; Luke 12:1; 1 Timothy 4:1-2;

In 1 Peter Chapter 2 we see the Lord stipulating that one of the criterions for receiving the Pure Word of God is that one must lay aside or put away any form of hypocrisy.

> "Therefore, laying aside all malice, all guile, hypocrisy, envy, and all evil speaking, [2]as newborn babes, desire the pure milk of the word, that you may grow thereby, [3]if indeed you have tasted that the Lord is gracious." 1 Peter 2:1-3

In Galatians Chapter 2 we read of a major dissention between the Apostles Paul and Peter, because of Peter's hypocrisy when in the company of the Jews. That hypocrisy threatened to destroy their relationship, hence the Apostle Paul had to effectively deal with it by confronting Peter and taking up the matter with him.

There is one other Greek word "anupokritos", which is rendered "without hypocrisy." The Scriptures encourage us to be in sync with this word. In James 3:17, we are encouraged to seek the Lord for His Wisdom, the one that comes from above and that is without hypocrisy:

> "Who is wise and understanding among you? Let him show by good conduct that his works are done in the meekness of wisdom. [14]But if you have bitter envy and self-seeking in your hearts, do not boast and lie against the truth. [15]This wisdom does not descend from above, but is earthly, sensual, demonic. [16]For where envy and self-seeking exist, confusion and every evil thing are there. [17]But the wisdom that is from above is first pure, then peaceable, gentle, willing to yield, full of mercy and good fruits, without partiality and without hypocrisy. [18]Now the fruit of righteousness is sown in peace by those who make peace." James 3:13-18

In the Book of Romans we are encouraged to let the foundation of our lives and ministry be that of *"Love without hypocrisy"*:

> "Let love be without hypocrisy. Abhor what is evil. Cling to what is good. [10]Be kindly affectionate to one another with brotherly love, in honour giving preference to one another; [11]not lagging in diligence, fervent in spirit, serving the Lord; [12]rejoicing in hope, patient in tribulation, continuing steadfastly in prayer; [13]distributing to the needs of the saints, given to hospitality. [14]Bless those who persecute you; bless and do not curse. [15]Rejoice with those who rejoice, and weep with those who weep. [16]Be of the same mind toward one another. Do not set your mind on high things, but associate with the humble. Do not be wise in your own opinion. [17]Repay no one evil for evil. Have regard for good things in the

sight of all men. [18]If it is possible, as much as depends on you, live peaceably with all men. [19]Beloved, do not avenge yourselves, but rather give place to wrath; for it is written, "Vengeance is Mine, I will repay," says the Lord. [20]Therefore "If your enemy is hungry, feed him; If he is thirsty, give him a drink; For in so doing you will heap coals of fire on his head." [21]Do not be overcome by evil, but overcome evil with good." Romans 12:9-21

As was alluded to earlier the leaven of the Pharisees is more than hypocrisy and erroneous doctrine. It goes a little further in its scope and extends to the corruption caused by the love of money.

The Pharisees had an excessive taste for riches and devoted excessive attention to business in order to secure those riches, and an abundance of goods. Jesus Christ's parable of the shrewd manager on the issue of stewardship as recorded by Apostle Luke is one of the best examples of this:

> "Whoever can be trusted with very little can also be trusted with much, and whoever is dishonest with very little will also be dishonest with much. [11]So if you have not been trustworthy in handling worldly wealth, who will trust you with true riches? [12]And if you have not been trustworthy with someone else's property, who will give you property of your own? [13]"No servant can serve two masters. Either he will hate the one and love the other, or he will be devoted to the one and despise the other. *You cannot serve both God and Money.*" [14]The *Pharisees, who loved money,* heard all this and were sneering [or mocking] at Jesus. [15]He said to them, "You are the ones who justify yourselves in the eyes of men, but God knows your hearts. What is highly valued among men is detestable in God's sight." [Italics and parenthesis added] Luke 16:10-15

The Pharisees controlled the Temple grounds and "made merchandize" of the people by selling doves [a poor persons offering] for the sacrifice at excessive prices. Jesus Christ had to drive the moneychangers from the Temple when He walked the earth and sadly, even in our modern churches, the Saints invite these charlatans in and support them.

We see much craziness where the "man or woman of God" declare that if we sow a certain amount of money [and it is usually a good sum] that the Lord would release them to pray a special prayer for material prosperity over the giver. Others propel the notion that a certain sum will release a special prophetic anointing that will culminate in a special word from God for the giver, and the list goes on and on. The Pharisees also grew their riches through their religion as it was extremely profitable, and nobody confronted them on these practices.

The charlatans in the Church need to be confronted on these side-show tactics. Simon the Sorcerer tried to buy the anointing and he found out that it was not for sale the hard way.

"But there was a certain *man called Simon*, who previously *practiced sorcery* in the city and astonished the people of Samaria, claiming that he was someone great, [10]to whom they all gave heed, from the least to the greatest, saying, "This man is the great power of God." [11]And they heeded him because he had astonished them with his sorceries for a long time. [12]But when they believed Philip as he preached the things concerning the kingdom of God and the name of Jesus Christ, both men and women were baptized. [13]*Then Simon himself also believed; and when he was baptized* he continued with Philip, *and was amazed, seeing the miracles and signs which were done.* [14]Now *when the apostles* who were at Jerusalem heard that Samaria had received the word of God, they sent Peter and John to them, [15]who, when they had come down, *prayed for them that they might receive the Holy Spirit.* [16]For as yet He had fallen upon none of them. They had only been baptized in the name of the Lord Jesus. [17]Then *they laid hands on them, and they received the Holy Spirit.* [18]And *when Simon saw* that through the laying on of the apostles' hands the Holy Spirit was given, *he offered them money,* [19]saying, "Give *me this power also, that anyone on whom I lay hands may receive the Holy Spirit."* [20]But *Peter said* to him, *"Your money perish with you,* because *you thought that the gift of God could be purchased with money!* [21]You have neither part nor portion in this matter, for *your heart is not right in the sight of God.* [22]Repent therefore of this your wickedness, and pray God if perhaps the thought of your heart may be forgiven you. [23]For I see that *you are poisoned by bitterness and bound by iniquity."* [Italics added NKJV] Acts 8:9-23

Simon was operating under a false Apostolic authority [probably some kind of mind control], and bewitched the people. He performed some false, demonic signs and the people feared him. However, when the Kingdom of God was preached, the demonic powers were broken and the eyes of the people were opened and they gladly received the Word and were baptized.

In verse 20 in particular, we see how harshly his antics are dealt with, "Peter answered: "May your money perish with you, because you thought you could buy the gift of God with money!" His own love of gain sentenced him to death.

Phillip being an Evangelist needed Apostolic grace and impartation to take the people into the next level and as soon as Apostles Peter and John arrived, true miracles, signs and wonders were witnessed for the first time, including a visible, manifested evidence of several persons receiving the Holy Spirit through the laying on of the Apostles' hands.

At that point Simon tried merchandizing the Apostolic anointing and Peter rose up in true Apostolic purity and rebuked him, even though the Word of God stated that this man also believed and was baptized.

Even to this day many are still trafficking in the anointing. However, this true Apostolic dimension is returning to the Body of Christ as the Holy Spirit restores Apostles who will function in purity and not merchandize the anointing.

There are many "Simon the sorcerer" types in our modern day and it remains perplexing that so many Believers flock to their meetings and fall for such craziness. Though they claim Jesus Christ as their own, these Believers actually believe that they will prosper by sowing into these charlatans and their ministries. We need be ever vigilant to check their lives to ensure that we are not falling prey to the erroneous teaching that financial gain is a sign of true godliness. Remember the teaching of Jesus Christ when He said:

> "Do not store up for yourselves treasures on earth, where moth and rust destroy, and where thieves break in and steal. [20]But store up for yourselves treasures in heaven, where moth and rust do not destroy, and where thieves do not break in and steal. [21]For where your treasure is, there your heart will be also. [22]"The eye is the lamp of the body. If your eyes are good, your whole body will be full of light. [23]But if your eyes are bad, your whole body will be full of darkness. If then the light within you is darkness, how great is that darkness! [24]"No one can serve two masters. Either he will hate the one and love the other, or he will be devoted to the one and despise the other. You cannot serve both God and Money. [25]"Therefore I tell you, do not worry about your life, what you will eat or drink; or about your body, what you will wear. Is not life more important than food, and the body more important than clothes? [26]Look at the birds of the air; they do not sow or reap or store away in barns, and yet your heavenly Father feeds them. Are you not much more valuable than they? [27]Who of you by worrying can add a single hour to his life?" Matthew 6:19-27

The Merchandizing of God's People:
When we consider the word merchandize, we think of setting up products for the consumer in an attractive way to make a sale. But the Scriptures use the word merchandize in regards to people and how they are handled. The word is translated from several Hebrew and Greek words which we will consider over the next section of the text.

Hebrew words for merchandizing:

Cachar – it is from a root meaning *to travel around as a peddler*; and is translated thus in:

> "Thus says the LORD: "The labour of Egypt and *merchandize* of Cush And of the Sabeans, men of stature, Shall come over to you, and they shall be yours..." [Italics added NKJV] Isaiah 45:14

Amar – translated in the King James Version as *make merchandize of*, but in the Revised Version [British and American] *deal with as a slave*, or the Revised Version margin *deal with as a chattel*, in the following verses:

> "And it shall be, if thou have no delight in her, then thou shalt let her go whither she will; but thou shalt not sell her at all for money, thou shalt not make *merchandize* of her, because thou hast humbled her." [Italics added KJV] Deuteronomy 21:14

> "Then, if you have no delight in her, you shall let her go where she will; but *you shall not sell her for money, you shall not treat her as a slave*, since you have humiliated her." [Italics added RSV]

> "If a man be found stealing any of his brethren of the children of Israel, and maketh *merchandize* of him, or selleth him; then that thief shall die; and thou shalt put evil away from among you." [Italics added KJV] Deuteronomy 24:7

> "If a man is found stealing one of his brethren, the people of Israel, and if he *treats him as a slave or sells him*, then that thief shall die; so you shall purge the evil from the midst of you." [Italics added RSV]

Interestingly enough this is exactly how the Lord views those who trade in the anointing. Some ministers use people with the anointing as slaves, and merchandize them.

Apostle Peter in much of his writings echoes this same concept with the Greek words used for merchandize:

Emporion – is from a root meaning to *make merchandize of you* – treat you like a slave, as is used in:

> "But there arose false prophets also among the people, as among you also there shall be false teachers, who shall privily bring in destructive heresies, denying even the Master that bought them, bringing upon themselves swift destruction. ²And many shall follow their lascivious doings; by reason of whom the way of the truth shall be evil spoken of. ³And in covetousness shall they *with feigned words make merchandize of you:* whose sentence now from of old lingereth not, and their destruction slumbereth not." [Italics added ASV] 2 Peter 2:1-3

Jesus Christ used the very same word *Emporion* when He encountered the traffickers in the temple:

> "And he found in the temple those that sold oxen and sheep and doves, and the changers of money sitting: ¹⁵and he made a scourge of cords, and cast all out of the temple, both the sheep and the oxen; and he poured out the changers' money, and overthrew their tables; ¹⁶and to them that sold the doves he said, Take these things hence; *make not my Father's house a house of merchandize."* [Italics added ASV] John 2:14-16

Jesus Christ is still doing this very thing today in His Temple, the Church, as there are many who continue with this devious practice of merchandizing God's people. There are many that barter and trade the anointing as they will not go and preach the word of God if *"the price is not right"*. Let me make myself clear here. I know we are not to muzzle the ox that treads out the grain and the workman is indeed worthy of his wages etc. However, we need to understand that if we are to walk in the levels of purity that are being required in this hour, we have to leave our wages wholly up to the Holy Spirit. Let Him establish what we should or should not get, and let us get on with business at hand, which is to assist in bringing the Church to a place of predestined maturity and greatness in the earth.

Apostle Paul in writing to the Corinthian church declared:

"For we are not, as so many, *peddling* the word of God; but as of sincerity, but as from God, we speak in the sight of God in Christ." [Italics added NKJV] 2 Corinthians 2:17

Here the Greek word used for peddling is the word *"kapeeleuontes"* and it conveys the idea of those who sit in the marketplace buying and selling. This word also speaks of dealers in victuals and all sorts of wares, but was especially applied to retailers of wine, with whom adulteration and short measure were matters of course.

The moral application of this word was familiar in Classical Greek. Both Lucian and Plato, the Greek philosophers in their writings refer to this word "kapeeleuontes". Plato wrote: "Those who carry about the wares of knowledge, and make the rounds of the cities, and sell or retail them to any customer who is in want of them, praise them all alike; though I should not wonder if many of them were really ignorant of their effect upon the soul; and their customers equally ignorant, unless he who buys of them happens to be a physician of the soul" [Protagoras, 313].

We have to be so careful as to not blur the lines where this is concerned. I urge those called to the Apostolic Office or any leadership position in the Body of Christ to walk *in utmost purity* in this area. Remember Judas [the one who carried the money bag], sold Jesus Christ out at a great price and ended up losing his place amongst the *"Twelve Apostles of the Lamb"* – an awesome, powerful designation. If he who actually walked with Jesus Christ did it, Apostles and Ministers today are not without temptation. Also, it will do well for us to understand that one of the reasons that lucifer was cast out of heaven was because of his *merchandizing* as was attested to in the following Scriptural text:

"Thou wast perfect in thy ways from the day that thou wast created, till iniquity was found in thee. ¹⁶By the *multitude of thy merchandize* they have filled the midst of thee with violence, and thou hast sinned: therefore I will cast thee as profane out of the mountain of God: and I will destroy thee, O covering cherub, from the midst of the stones of fire. [17]Thine heart was lifted up because of thy beauty, thou hast corrupted thy wisdom by reason of thy brightness: I will cast thee to the ground, I will lay thee before kings, that they may behold thee. [18]Thou hast defiled thy sanctuaries by the multitude of thine iniquities, *by the iniquity of thy traffick*; therefore will I bring forth a fire from the midst of thee, it shall devour thee, and I will bring thee to ashes upon the earth in the sight of all them that behold thee." [Italics added KJV] Ezekiel 28:15-18

[3]Wealth is one of the pillars of the Apostolic dealt with in the author's book "Five Pillars of The Apostolic" and we will do well to understand that this wealth is not for individual Ministers or Ministries to exploit, but to be used in advancing God's Kingdom in the earth.

Isn't it interesting how Judas Iscariot the only Apostle out of the original Twelve lost his apostleship because of his love for money. He had a Pharisee devil, like several today who claim to be Apostles!

As we close this chapter, allow me to say that there is much more that can be and probably has been written on this subject. However, let me re-emphasize the fact that Jesus Christ strictly warned us to guard vehemently against having our lives contaminated and infected with the leaven of the Pharisees – this hypocrisy with deep roots and a solid foundation.

---

[3] You can read the author's book "Five Pillars of The Apostolic" for a more in-depth analysis of this pillar of the Apostolic; ordering details at the end of this book.

CHAPTER 5

THE LEAVEN OF THE SADDUCEES

The Sadducees were another priestly group and some Christians probably lump them together with the Pharisees as they are often mentioned together in the Bible. But the Sadducees were very different from the Pharisees as they were descendants of Aaron and associated with the leadership of the Temple in Jerusalem. Of note, during Jesus Christ's time on earth the religious/political group of the Sadducees was known for their liberalism. They were very aristocratic and tended to be very wealthy and held very powerful positions, such as that of high priest.

The Sadducees held the majority of the 70 seats of the ruling council known as the [4]Sanhedrin. They moved with the "upper class" of society and mirrored many of Rome's political maneuvers to gain strength and popularity among the Roman authorities. To their own advancement, they also worked very closely with the Pharisee minority in the Sanhedrin council as the Pharisees had the hearts of the common folk. This worked in tandem to their advantage as the Sadducees had the hearts of the affluent.

The Sadducees held fast to the written Word of God – especially the Pentateuch, which is comprised of Genesis through Deuteronomy and is also known as the Five Books of Moses.

---

[4] A variety of theories have developed concerning the Sanhedrin of Jewish leaders in Jerusalem. The three most prevalent are that the Sanhedrin was composed of political leaders, including some priests and aristocrats; that the Sanhedrin was composed of religious leaders knowledgeable in the law, including priests, Pharisees, and scribes; and that there were two Sanhedrins, one political and the other religious. Achtemeier, Paul J., Th.D., Harper's Bible Dictionary, (San Francisco: Harper and Row, Publishers, Inc.) 1985.

However, due to their extremely political bias they tended to compromise Scripture and adopted some erroneous doctrinal practices and beliefs. As a matter of fact these religious zealots of the day were the ones who with the Pharisees plotted to crucify Jesus Christ when their authority was severely being threatened by His teachings.

"Then the Pharisees and Sadducees came, and testing Him asked that He would show them a sign from heaven. [2]He answered and said to them, "When it is evening you say, 'It will be fair weather, for the sky is red'; [3]and in the morning, 'It will be foul weather today, for the sky is red and threatening.' Hypocrites! You know how to discern the face of the sky, but you cannot discern the signs of the times. [4]A wicked and adulterous generation seeks after a sign, and no sign shall be given to it except the sign of the prophet Jonah." And He left them and departed. [5]Now when His disciples had come to the other side, they had forgotten to take bread. [6]Then Jesus said to them, "Take heed and beware of the leaven of the Pharisees and the Sadducees." [7]And they reasoned among themselves, saying, "It is because we have taken no bread." [8]But Jesus, being aware of it, said to them, "O you of little faith, why do you reason among yourselves because you have brought no bread? [9]Do you not yet understand, or remember the five loaves of the five thousand and how many baskets you took up? [10]Nor the seven loaves of the four thousand and how many large baskets you took up? [11]How is it you do not understand that I did not speak to you concerning bread?–but to beware of the leaven of the Pharisees and Sadducees." [12]Then they understood that He did not tell them to beware of the leaven of bread, but of the doctrine of the Pharisees and Sadducees. Matthew 16:1-12

"The same day the Sadducees, *who say there is no resurrection*, came to Him with a question. [24]"Teacher," they said, "Moses told us that if a man dies without having children, his brother must marry the widow and have children for him. [25]Now there were seven brothers among us. The first one married and died, and since he had no children, he left his wife to his brother. ²⁶The same thing happened to the second and third brother, right on down to the seventh. ²⁷Finally, the woman died. ²⁸Now then, at the resurrection, whose wife will she be of the seven, since all of them were married to her?" ²⁹Jesus replied, "You are in error because you do not know the Scriptures or the power of God. ³⁰At the resurrection people will neither marry nor be given in marriage; they will be like the angels in heaven. ³¹But about the resurrection of the dead—have you not read what God said to you, ³²'I am the God of Abraham, the God of Isaac, and the God of Jacob'? He is not the God of the dead but of the living." ³³When the crowds heard this, they were astonished at his teaching." [Italics added] Matthew 22:23-33

According to Matthew 16:1-12 and Matthew 22:23 The Sadducees did not believe in the resurrection of the dead or the immortality of the soul, yet they question Jesus Christ on aspects of the Scripture denoting the resurrection. They were conniving all the while to trap Jesus Christ!

They did not believe in rewards or punishments being handed out after death. Hence they denied the doctrines of heaven and hell. The Sadducees were legalists and held their people in bondage to the Law.

I believe that there were four main areas of leaven or contradictions to Scripture that the Sadducees functioned in that we need to be aware of. They are:

- They denied the Resurrection of the dead.

- They denied the existence of angels and demons – Acts 23:6-8.

- They denied life after death, proclaiming that the soul perished at death and as such there was neither reward, nor penalty for things done in one's earthly life.

- They were very self-centered and self-sufficient and as such denied the Lord's involvement in their day-to-day lives.

Of the four main areas of error/leaven that the Sadducees subscribed to, their unbelief in the Resurrection of the dead was the most deadly and as such we will need to explore this aspect in a bit more detail.

The Resurrection Of The Dead:
This is a very elaborate and extensive study and the scope of this writing is not intended to explore such depth. However, as we briefly touch on this subject let me state that the Resurrection is one of the foundational pillars of the Gospel and the Christian Church!

The Resurrection was so important that it was one of the main topics of the early Apostles' teachings. When they preached they always testified concerning the Resurrection of Jesus Christ, and the consequent resurrection of the dead. As a matter of fact the Resurrection of Jesus Christ in bodily form was so important that when the remaining Eleven Apostles had to chose another Apostle to replace Judas Iscariot who had became apostate, they knew that the replacement had to have witnessed the Resurrection of Jesus Christ.

> "In those days Peter stood up among the believers (a group numbering about a hundred and twenty) [16]and said, "Brothers, the Scripture had to be fulfilled which the Holy Spirit spoke long ago through the mouth of David concerning Judas, who served as guide for those who arrested Jesus— [17]he was one of our number and shared in this ministry." [18](With the reward he got for his wickedness, Judas bought a field; there he fell headlong, his body burst open and all his intestines spilled out. [19]Everyone in Jerusalem heard about this, so they called that field in their language Akeldama, that is, Field of Blood.) [20]"For," said Peter, "it is written in the book of Psalms, " 'May his place be deserted; let there be no one to dwell in it,' and," 'May another take his place of leadership.' [21]Therefore it is necessary to choose one of the

men who have been with us the whole time the Lord
Jesus went in and out among us, [22]beginning from John's
baptism to the time when Jesus was taken up from us. *For
one of these must become a witness with us of his
resurrection.*" [23]So they proposed two men: Joseph called
Barsabbas (also known as Justus) and Matthias. [24]Then
they prayed, "Lord, you know everyone's heart. Show us
which of these two you have chosen [25]to take over this
apostolic ministry, which Judas left to go where he
belongs." [26]Then they cast lots, and the lot fell to Matthias;
so he was added to the eleven apostles." [Italics added]
Acts 1:15-26

From that time the Apostles continued to preach very strongly
concerning the Resurrection of the dead. We see this in the
following Scriptural texts:

When Apostle Peter stood up before the multitude, he declared
unto them that "David spoke of the Resurrection of Jesus Christ."
When Peter and John were taken before the council, after healing
the man at the Temple gate, the great cause of their arrest was not
because of that healing as some may suppose. No, the rulers
were grieved because they propagated the teachings of Jesus
Christ including the Resurrection from the dead.

"The priests and the captain of the temple guard and the
Sadducees came up to Peter and John while they were
speaking to the people. [2]They were greatly disturbed
because the apostles were teaching the people and
proclaiming in Jesus the resurrection of the dead. [3]They
seized Peter and John, and because it was evening, they
put them in jail until the next day." Acts 4:1-3

Even the caging of Peter and John as criminals in a common jail
did not diminish the Apostles' fervour about preaching on the
resurrection from the dead. When they were set free, after having
been examined, they returned to the brethren and gave their
report as we read in the following: "[23]On their release, Peter and
John went back to their own people and reported all that the chief

priests and elders had said to them... [33]With great power the apostles continued to testify to the resurrection of the Lord Jesus, and much grace was upon them all." Acts 4:23, 33.

It was the resurrection which stirred the curiosity of the Athenians when Apostle Paul preached among them:

> "While Paul was waiting for them in Athens, he was greatly distressed to see that the city was full of idols. [17]So he reasoned in the synagogue with the Jews and the God-fearing Greeks, as well as in the marketplace day by day with those who happened to be there. [18]A group of Epicurean and Stoic philosophers began to dispute with him. Some of them asked, "What is this babbler trying to say?" Others remarked, "He seems to be advocating foreign gods." They said this because Paul was preaching the good news *about Jesus and the resurrection*. Then they took him and brought him to a meeting of the Areopagus, where they said to him, "May we know what this new teaching is that you are presenting?" [Italics added] Acts 17:16-19

In response to them the Apostle Paul preached the Gospel with fervour and ended on the note concerning the Resurrection of the dead. This moved the Areopagites to respond in a scornful and contemptuous manner, as we see in the following Scriptural reference:

> "When they heard about the resurrection of the dead, some of them sneered, but others said, "We want to hear you again on this subject." Acts 4:32

As the Apostle Paul was nearing the end of his life on earth, he was arrested in Jerusalem and was brought before the Sanhedrin Council as Rome could not find any fault with him. Remember that Apostle Paul was a Roman citizen and ill treatment of a Roman citizen could have serious consequences on the person making the allegations and imposing the sentence.

> "Those who were about to question him withdrew immediately. The commander himself was alarmed when

he realized that he had put Paul, a Roman citizen, in chains.[30]The next day, since the commander wanted to find out exactly why Paul was being accused by the Jews, he released him and ordered the chief priests and all the Sanhedrin to assemble. Then he brought Paul and had him stand before them." Acts 22:29-30

Without fear of man, not even the ruling party of the Sanhedrin Council and the high priest, he rose up in only the way Apostle Paul could and stated the following:

"Paul looked straight at the Sanhedrin and said, "My brothers, I have fulfilled my duty to God in all good conscience to this day." ...[6]Then Paul, knowing that some of them were Sadducees and the others Pharisees, called out in the Sanhedrin, "My brothers, I am a Pharisee, the son of a Pharisee. *I stand on trial because of my hope in the resurrection of the dead.*" [7]When he said this, a dispute broke out between the Pharisees and the Sadducees, and the assembly was divided. [8](The Sadducees say that there is no resurrection, and that there are neither angels nor spirits, but the Pharisees acknowledge them all.)" [Italics added] Acts 23:1, 6-8

When we speak about the Resurrection of the dead we are not speaking about one's spirit or soul as these are already eternal. However, our physical body [the body consisting of flesh, blood and bones] in the current state is NOT eternal.

As we study Scripture we would all have to agree that regardless to our doctrinal position one thing is certain, God's original plan was and still is, His desire and ultimate goal to have earth populated with mankind [by mankind we mean, a being with a spirit and a soul who live in a body of flesh]. We are not going to live in Heaven. God never intended for mankind to live in Heaven. It was and still is His desire and intent for us to live on planet earth! However having said that, in order for that to be accomplished we must have bodies that can fulfill that objective, hence the reason for the Resurrection. Our current bodies will have to put on immortality in order for us [spirit and soul] to live forever on planet earth.

Let me once again re-emphasize that the Resurrection is not a simple concept or occurrence, it is the very basis for the Christian Faith. The Old Testament Saints believed in it and longed and looked forward for it. The Book of Hebrews records a powerful point in support of this when the writer penned the following by the inspiration of the Holy Spirit:

> "Now faith is being sure of what we hope for and certain of what we do not see. [2]This is what the ancients were commended for... [13]All these people were still living by faith when they died. They did not receive the things promised; they only saw them and welcomed them from a distance. And they admitted that they were aliens and strangers on earth. [14]People who say such things show that they are looking for a country of their own. [15]If they had been thinking of the country they had left, they would have had opportunity to return. [16]Instead, they were longing for a better country—a heavenly one. Therefore God is not ashamed to be called their God, for he has prepared a city for them... [20]By faith Isaac blessed Jacob and Esau in regard to their future. [21]By faith Jacob, when he was dying, blessed each of Joseph's sons, and worshiped as he leaned on the top of his staff. *[22]By faith Joseph, when his end was near, spoke about the exodus of the Israelites from Egypt and gave instructions about his bones...* [32]And what more shall I say? I do not have time to tell about Gideon, Barak, Samson, Jephthah, David, Samuel and the prophets, [33]who through faith conquered kingdoms, administered justice, and gained what was promised; who shut the mouths of lions, [34]quenched the fury of the flames, and escaped the edge of the sword; whose weakness was turned to strength; and who became powerful in battle and routed foreign armies. [35]Women received back their dead, raised to life again. Others were tortured and refused to be released, so that they might gain a better resurrection. [36]Some faced jeers and flogging,

while still others were chained and put in prison. [37]They were stoned; they were sawed in two; they were put to death by the sword. They went about in sheepskins and goatskins, destitute, persecuted and mistreated— [38]the world was not worthy of them. They wandered in deserts and mountains, and in caves and holes in the ground. [39]These were all commended for their faith, yet none of them received what had been promised. [40]God had planned something better for us so that only together with us would they be made perfect. [Italics added] Hebrews 11:1-2, 13-40

[5]Verse 22 reveals that – By faith Joseph, when his end was near, spoke about the exodus of the Israelites from Egypt and gave instructions about his bones – therein lies one of the most powerful truths concerning the Resurrection. Instruction about the care of a person's bones seems like a strange thing to record about a man in Hebrews Chapter 11, known as the Faith Chapter in Scripture. It makes you wonder why Joseph's bones were mentioned at all. After all, the Chapter speaks to the faith of the Patriarchs and the hurdles they had to pass through. So, what does the mention of a dead person's bones have to do with faith? To fully understand this we need to briefly retrace the life of this great Patriarch along with some of his Kinsmen.

The entire 23rd Chapter of Genesis deals with Abraham purchasing a cave for the burial of his wife and family. The resting place for the remains of his relatives was very important and sacred to Abraham. Sarah died and it was time to provide a final resting place for his loved ones. Abraham refused to take it as a gift and required that the deal be signed and sealed so that future generations could not deny that this place belonged to Abraham and his heirs.

Abraham, the Bible says, was a Prophet and through the eyes of faith, he saw the future unfold. He knew that one day, the very land he was adamant in purchasing as a burial ground would belong to

---

[5] Adapted from the book Reach for the Stars -The Bones of Joseph, by Bill Britton
    http://www.dimensionsoftruth.org/Bill_Britton/reach_stars03.html

the tribe of Judah, just a few miles south of Jerusalem, the Holy City.

Later on in time Jacob, Abraham's grandson is about to die and he calls all his sons to himself and instructs and blesses them before his departure as recorded in Genesis:

> "Then he gave them these instructions: "I am about to be gathered to my people. Bury me with my fathers in the cave in the field of Ephron the Hittite, [30] the cave in the field of Machpelah, near Mamre in Canaan, which Abraham bought as a burial place from Ephron the Hittite, along with the field. [31] There Abraham and his wife Sarah were buried, there Isaac and his wife Rebekah were buried, and there I buried Leah. [32] The field and the cave in it were bought from the Hittites." Genesis 49:29-32

Abraham's cave at Machpelah not only held the remains of Abraham and Sarah buried there, but also Isaac, Rebekah, Jacob and Leah. They all rested in this place and now, much later in time and a long ways away in the land of Egypt we find Joseph giving instructions for his bones to be taken out with the children of Israel when God brought them out of Egypt. He declared to the Israelites:

> "Then Joseph said to his brothers, "I am about to die. But God will surely come to your aid and take you up out of this land to the land he promised on oath to Abraham, Isaac and Jacob." [25]And Joseph made the sons of Israel swear an oath and said, "*God will surely come to your aid, and then you must carry my bones up from this place.*" [26]So Joseph died at the age of a hundred and ten. And after they embalmed him, he was placed in a coffin in Egypt." [Italics added] Genesis 50:24-26

Joseph died and his body was embalmed and placed in a tomb in Egypt for hundreds of years. The Children of Israel continued in their hellish bondage and one has to pose the question as to how many of them really believed Joseph's prophetic insight in declaring that they would be liberated. Hundreds of years passed and his prophecy that declared that God would bring them out should have given them incredible faith and hope.

"And Moses took the bones of Joseph with Him." Exodus 13:19

He was taking no chances. The Word of God had been spoken, and an oath had been taken. Moses knew that the impossible task before him could only be met through the Word of God. His strength and abilities were as nothing in the face of the problem, but this coffin of bones was his insurance. Joseph, the Prophet of God, had spoken the word. And Moses stood on the word of God.

The Resurrection was so important to Joseph that his body remained in a tomb in Egypt for over 400 years and then was transported through the wilderness for another 40 years before finally coming to rest in the Promised Land.

One may ask what difference could it possibly make to Joseph where his dead body rested? The answer is that he was a very spiritual man, and as long as he knew his spirit would be with his Lord, why was he so concerned about his flesh? It was far more than just a sentimental gesture. There was a deep spiritual significance.

Joseph was a Prophet, a Seer, one who sees future events. And he saw a glorious event taking place more than seventeen centuries after his death. He saw the glory that would come to those who would be able to participate in this great event, and he wanted to be a part of it. Hear me beloved, for this concerns you today. The Spirit of God showed this man a glory that was coming. But there was something he had to do. He made arrangements for his body to be buried just south of the city of Jerusalem, in a cave purchased for that very purpose. He made provisions to be in the place where he could participate in the greatest event ever where Jesus Christ gave Himself to be a blood sacrifice to redeem us from sin and Joseph knew that many years hence, he too would partake in that glory.

This wonderful event is recorded in the Gospel of Matthew:

> "And when Jesus had cried out again in a loud voice, he gave up his spirit. [51]At that moment the curtain of the temple was torn in two from top to bottom. The earth shook and the rocks split. [52]The tombs broke open and

the bodies of many holy people who had died were
raised to life. [53]They came out of the tombs, and after Jesus'
resurrection they went into the holy city and appeared
to many people." Matthew 27:51-53

What a world shaking, history-making thing was taking place!
Jesus Christ had been crucified, had paid the penalty for our sins,
and on the third day had risen from the tomb. Matthew reports
that the moment Jesus Christ cried out with a loud voice and died
that the veil in the Old Covenant Temple was torn from top to
bottom [signifying the end to the old system], and that many
Saints who previously died and were buried, were resurrected.
And for three days they remained alive in their tombs. Then,
following His resurrection, graves of many of the saints were
opened and they came into the city. Although the Scriptures do
not specify the names of all who were resurrected, I am confident
that some of them were mentioned in Hebrews Chapter 11.
Possibly Joseph was among those who were resurrected!

It states that "They went into the city," so it stands to reason that
the graves were somewhere outside the city. It does not say
where the graves were, but I know of one that was located in a
cave somewhere south of Jerusalem, which I am confident you
would find empty if you went there today. They "appeared unto
many." It does not say they were recognized, but they were seen.
They were not seen as spirits or ghosts, not as dried up piles of
bones rattling down the streets of Jerusalem, but they were seen
in their bodies, their new bodies, their *resurrected, glorified
bodies*. And nowhere does it say, and it would be a violation of
Scripture and reason to even imagine that those Saints returned to
their old graves and died again or returned to dust.

I believe with all my heart that the Prophet Joseph was among
those who walked the streets of Jerusalem that day, as well as
Abraham, Isaac, and Jacob. Why else did the Spirit lead them to
make their burial place certain, almost on the outskirts of that city
where all this was taking place? So what is the result? Many bodies
of Saints, including all the New Testament Church who have
gone on to be with the Lord are still in the grave today, waiting for

the Resurrection. Then shall they be clothed upon with life, and then shall death be swallowed up in victory! This is our inheritance as Saints, and we are looking ever onward to that blessed hope.

But there were some who did not have to wait until the final trump for their corruptible bodies to put on incorruptible. Up to now, they have been enjoying their glorified bodies for almost 2000 years. Why? Because they were men and women of faith, Saints, "set apart."

Consider again Joseph. While he had the authority, he made them take an oath so binding upon Israel that in spite of the difficulties involved, they had to carry his bones through 40 years of wilderness wanderings until they could put him to rest in the Cave. By the eye of the Spirit he not only saw the departure of the Children of Israel from Egypt, but he also saw a greater event and made sure that he would be near enough to be a part of it.

The important thing about this whole message is how it affects us today in this end of the age. I want you to see the glorious thing that God is about to do in the earth in our time. The Saints who arose with Jesus Christ were the first-fruits of the Resurrection. They are living proof that the harvest is actually going to follow. We do not have to fear that this glorious promise of life after death is only a myth or fable. Jesus Christ Himself with many of the Saints actually arose and walked the streets of Jerusalem in their new bodies and were seen by the people. This was the first-fruits, but the harvest was to wait for many centuries. Joseph did not have to wait; he could be in the first-fruits company, because of his vision, his desire, and his faith. God has promised that the "latter house shall be greater than the former."

Let the bones of Joseph speak to your heart; he [well his bones] spent over 1700 years in a tomb waiting for the coming of Messiah to come, to die, be buried and to rise again from the dead so that he could have experienced the First Resurrection or to be among the First-Fruits of them who slept. Well there still remains a Resurrection of the body for those Saints who have died and will die before Jesus Christ returns to finally setup His Throne and headquarters upon planet earth!

I believe that there is a final Resurrection still to be accomplished. Some will be resurrected to eternal damnation and others to eternal life and bliss. Even though we have been waiting a little under 2000 years to see this happen, I am here to tell you that it certainly will happen!

There are some who have been locked into this doctrine of the Sadducees and are denying any resurrection to come. However, there must be a final Resurrection as God will come and permanently live upon the earth!

When Jesus Christ came in the flesh the first time, He came as Saviour to die for the sins of the world. At that time the Jews wanted Him to set up His Kingdom with them and overthrow the Roman rule. He rejected that as He was on a mission to die for the sins of the world. However, when He returns He will be coming as King of His Kingdom to reign forever in the earth.

There is so much more that can be said about the Resurrection, that it will take many, many more books to completely deal with this all-important pillar of the Christian Faith. However, I would like to leave you with the following all-important passage from one of Apostle Paul's letters to the Corinthian church concerning the Resurrection:

> "Now, brothers, I want to remind you of the gospel I preached to you, which you received and on which you have taken your stand. [2]By this gospel you are saved, if you hold firmly to the word I preached to you. Otherwise, you have believed in vain. [3]For what I received I passed on to you as of first importance: that Christ died for our sins according to the Scriptures, [4]that he was buried, that he was raised on the third day according to the Scriptures, [5]and that he appeared to Peter, and then to the Twelve. [6]After that, he appeared to more than five hundred of the brothers at the same time, most of whom are still living, though some have fallen asleep. [7]Then he appeared to

James, then to all the apostles, [8]and last of all he appeared to me also, as to one abnormally born. [9]For I am the least of the apostles and do not even deserve to be called an apostle, because I persecuted the church of God. [10]But by the grace of God I am what I am, and his grace to me was not without effect. No, I worked harder than all of them—yet not I, but the grace of God that was with me. [11]Whether, then, it was I or they, this is what we preach, and this is what you believed. [12]*But if it is preached that Christ has been raised from the dead, how can some of you say that there is no resurrection of the dead?* [13]*If there is no resurrection of the dead, then not even Christ has been raised.* [14]And if Christ has not been raised, our preaching is useless and so is your faith. [15]More than that, we are then found to be false witnesses about God, for we have testified about God that he raised Christ from the dead. But he did not raise him if in fact the dead are not raised. [16]*For if the dead are not raised, then Christ has not been raised either.* [17]And if Christ has not been raised, your faith is futile; you are still in your sins. [18]*Then those also who have fallen asleep in Christ are lost.* [19]If only for this life we have hope in Christ, we are to be pitied more than all men. [20]But Christ has indeed been raised from the dead, the first-fruits of those who have fallen asleep. [21]For since death came through a man, the resurrection of the dead comes also through a man. [22]For as in Adam all die, so in Christ all will be made alive. [23]But each in his own turn: Christ, the first-fruits; then, when he comes, those who belong to him. [24]Then the end will come, when he hands over the kingdom to God the Father after he has destroyed all dominion, authority and power. [25]For he must reign until he has put all his enemies under his feet. [26]The last enemy to be destroyed is death. [27]For he "has put everything under his feet." Now when it says that "everything" has been put under him, it is clear that this does not include God himself, who put everything under Christ. [28]When he has done this, then the Son himself will be made subject to him who put everything under him, so that God may be all in all. ²⁹Now if there is no resurrection, what will those do who are baptized for the dead? If the dead are not raised at all, why are people baptized for them? ³⁰And as for us, why do we endanger ourselves every hour? ³¹I die every day—I mean that, brothers—just as surely as I glory over you in Christ Jesus our Lord. ³²If I fought wild beasts in Ephesus for merely human reasons, what have I gained? If the dead are not raised, "Let us eat and drink, for tomorrow we die." ³³Do not be misled: "Bad company corrupts good character." ³⁴Come back to your senses as you ought, and stop sinning; for there are some who are ignorant of God—I say this to your shame. ³⁵But someone may ask, "How are the dead raised? With what kind of body will they come?" ³⁶How foolish! What you sow does not come to life unless it dies. ³⁷When you sow, you do not plant the body that will be, but just a seed, perhaps of wheat or of something else. ³⁸But God gives it a body as he has determined, and to each kind of seed he gives its own body. ³⁹All flesh is not the same: Men have one kind of flesh, animals have another, birds another and fish another. ⁴⁰There are also heavenly bodies and there are earthly bodies; but the splendour of the heavenly bodies is one kind, and the splendour of the earthly bodies is another. ⁴¹The sun has one kind of splendour, the moon another and the stars another; and star differs from star in splendour. ⁴²*So will it be with the resurrection of the dead. The body that is sown is perishable, it is raised imperishable;* ⁴³*it is sown in dishonour, it is raised in glory; it is sown in weakness, it is raised in power;* ⁴⁴*it is sown a natural body, it is raised a spiritual body. If there is a natural body, there is also a spiritual body.* ⁴⁵So it is written: "The first man Adam became a living being"; the last Adam, a life-giving spirit. ⁴⁶The spiritual did not come first, but the natural, and after that the spiritual. ⁴⁷The first man was of the dust of the earth, the second man from heaven. ⁴⁸As was the earthly man, so are those who are of the earth; and as is the man from heaven, so also are those who are of heaven.

[49]And just as we have borne the likeness of the earthly man, so shall we bear the likeness of the man from heaven. [50]I declare to you, brothers, that flesh and blood cannot inherit the kingdom of God, nor does the perishable inherit the imperishable. [51]Listen, I tell you a mystery: We will not all sleep, but we will all be changed— [52]in a flash, in the twinkling of an eye, at the last trumpet. For the trumpet will sound, the dead will be raised imperishable, and we will be changed. [53]*For the perishable must clothe itself with the imperishable, and the mortal with immortality.* [54]*When the perishable has been clothed with the imperishable, and the mortal with immortality, then the saying that is written will come true: "Death has been swallowed up in victory."* [55]"Where, O death, is your victory? Where, O death, is your sting?" [56]The sting of death is sin, and the power of sin is the law. [57]But thanks be to God! He gives us the victory through our Lord Jesus Christ. [58]Therefore, my dear brothers, stand firm. Let nothing move you. Always give yourselves fully to the work of the Lord, because you know that your labour in the Lord is not in vain." [Italics added] 1 Corinthians 15:1-58

As we have seen in this chapter, the Sadducees were legalists and held their people in bondage to the Law with no hope in the promises of Scripture. This proved to be a very powerful control tactic to the religious faithful who succumbed to tradition and who did not have independent thoughts on the matter. The leaven of the Sadducees was "legalism and unbelief in the Resurrection", and in their day, they managed to have it leaven and corrupt the whole loaf of the Jewish society, but only until Jesus Christ arrived!

CHAPTER 6

THE LEAVEN OF THE GALATIANS

The territory in modern central Turkey known as Galatia was an oddity in the Eastern world. It was originally home of the ancient civilization of the Hittites, but came to be occupied by Gallic Celts in the 3rd century BC, hence Galatia, or "Gallia of the East." Galatia also became an early stronghold for the Christian church. The Apostle Paul visited the province around 55 AD and wrote his Epistle to the Galatians. The Celts apparently took to his teaching in earnest and the early church spread and flourished.

However, it was not long after the establishment of a strong church in Galatia that major problems surfaced due to erroneous doctrine that was introduced with the intent of completely destroying the church. Because of this chaotic influence of false doctrine permeating the church, the Apostle Paul wrote a very significant and serious letter to the Galatians. The entire Epistle was written to counteract the leavening influence of a few Judaizers [Believers who mixed the rituals of Judaism with their Christian faith] who had come amongst the Galatians, and were endeavouring to persuade them that in order to be perfect Christians it was necessary to be circumcised and to observe the Law of Moses.

In order to effectively refute the debilitating effect of their leaven, Apostle Paul began his apologetic first by defending his Apostolic authority by proving that God called him and imparted the truth of the Gospel to him by means of a direct revelation. Secondly, Apostle Paul aggressively exposed the leaven of the Judaizers. He knew it was incumbent on him to expose this leaven and its errors that were leading the Galatians astray.

Apostle Paul's fervor and the commitment to truth is evident in his letter to the Galatians:

"Paul, an apostle—sent not from men nor by man, but by Jesus Christ and God the Father, who raised him from the dead— [2]and all the brothers with me, To the churches in Galatia: [3]Grace and peace to you from God our Father and the Lord Jesus Christ, [4]who gave himself for our sins to rescue us from the present evil age, according to the will of our God and Father, [5]to whom be glory for ever and ever. Amen. [6]I am astonished that you are so quickly deserting the one who called you by the grace of Christ and are turning to a different gospel— [7]which is really no gospel at all. Evidently some people are throwing you into confusion and are trying to pervert the gospel of Christ. [8]But even if we or an angel from heaven should preach a gospel other than the one we preached to you, let him be eternally condemned! [9]As we have already said, so now I say again: If anybody is preaching to you a gospel other than what you accepted, let him be eternally condemned! [10]Am I now trying to win the approval of men, or of God? Or am I trying to please men? If I were still trying to please men, I would not be a servant of Christ. [11]I want you to know, brothers, that the gospel I preached is not something that man made up. [12]I did not receive it from any man, nor was I taught it; rather, I received it by revelation from Jesus Christ. [13]For you have heard of my previous way of life in Judaism, how intensely I persecuted the church of God and tried to destroy it. [14]I was advancing in Judaism beyond many Jews of my own age and was extremely zealous for the traditions of my fathers. [15]But when God, who set me apart from birth and called me by his grace, was pleased [16]to reveal his Son in me so that I might preach him among the Gentiles, I did not consult any man, [17]nor did I go up to Jerusalem to see those who were apostles before I was, but I went immediately into Arabia and later returned to Damascus. [18]Then after three years, I went up to Jerusalem to get acquainted with Peter and stayed with him fifteen days. [19]I saw none of the other apostles—only James, the

Lord's brother. [20]I assure you before God that what I am writing you is no lie. [21]Later I went to Syria and Cilicia. [22]I was personally unknown to the churches of Judea that are in Christ. [23]They only heard the report: "The man who formerly persecuted us is now preaching the faith he once tried to destroy." [24]And they praised God because of me." Galatians 1:1-24

There were several issues that Apostle Paul had to deal with as he sought to get the churches of Galatia back on track. While this tome is not intended to deal in detail with every issue that the Apostle Paul addressed, it would be beneficial that we list every issue so as to gain a more comprehensive understanding of the ills of the Galatians' church:

1. He warned the Galatians that they received the Holy Spirit by believing in Jesus Christ, even before they knew about the Law from the Judaizers.

    "You foolish Galatians! Who has bewitched you? Before your very eyes Jesus Christ was clearly portrayed as crucified. [2]I would like to learn just one thing from you: Did you receive the Spirit by observing the law, or by believing what you heard? [3]Are you so foolish? After beginning with the Spirit, are you now trying to attain your goal by human effort? [4]Have you suffered so much for nothing—if it really was for nothing? [5]Does God give you his Spirit and work miracles among you because you observe the law, or because you believe what you heard?" Galatians 3:1-5

2. He further explained to them that God's blessing of Abraham's faith was extended to all nations – through Jesus Christ, and was no longer exclusive to the Jews, Abraham's natural race.

    "Consider Abraham: "He believed God, and it was credited to him as righteousness." [7]Understand, then, that those who believe are children of Abraham. [8]The Scripture foresaw that God would justify the Gentiles by faith, and announced the gospel in advance to Abraham: "All nations will be blessed through you." [9]So those who have faith are blessed along with Abraham, the man of faith. [10]All who rely on observing the law are under a curse, for it is written: "Cursed is everyone who does not continue to do everything written in the Book of the Law." [11]Clearly no one is justified before God by the law, because, "The righteous will live by faith." [12]The law is not based on faith; on the contrary, "The man who does these things will live by them." [13]Christ redeemed us from the curse of the law by becoming a curse for us, for it is written: "Cursed is everyone who is hung on a tree." [14]He redeemed us in order that the blessing given to Abraham might come to the Gentiles through Christ Jesus, so that by faith we might receive the promise of the Spirit." Galatians 3:6-14

3. He reiterated the fact that God's promises to Abraham, were established long before the Law, and are fulfilled in Jesus Christ. Also he taught that the Law had been there to act as a "custodian or disciplinarian" until Jesus Christ came!

"Brothers, let me take an example from everyday life. Just as no one can set aside or add to a human covenant that has been duly established, so it is in this case. [16]The promises were spoken to Abraham and to his seed. The Scripture does not say "and to seeds," meaning many people, but "and to your seed," meaning one person, who is Christ. [17]What I mean is this: The law, introduced 430 years later, does not set aside the covenant previously established by God and thus do away with the promise. [18]For if the inheritance depends on the law, then it no longer depends on a promise; but God in his grace gave it to Abraham through a promise. [19]What, then, was the purpose of the law? It was added because of transgressions until the Seed to whom the promise referred had come. The law was put into effect through angels by a mediator. [20]A mediator, however, does not represent just one party; but God is one. [21]Is the law, therefore, opposed to the promises of God? Absolutely not! For if a law had been given that could impart life, then righteousness would certainly have come by the law. [22]But the Scripture declares that the whole world is a prisoner of sin, so that what was promised, being given through faith in Jesus Christ, might be given to those who believe. [23]Before this faith came, we were held prisoners by the law, locked up until faith should be revealed. [24]So the law was put in charge to lead us to Christ that we might be justified by faith. [25]Now that faith has come, we are no longer under the supervision of the law." Galatians 3:15-25

4. He broke the elitist spirit of the Judaizers who wanted to lord it over the Galatians that they were the chosen few who truly had "it." Apostle Paul clearly showed the Galatians that every Believer who was no longer a slave to the "elemental spirits" of the world is a Son of God:

"You are all sons of God through faith in Christ Jesus, [27]for all of you who were baptized into Christ have clothed yourselves with Christ. [28]There is neither Jew nor Greek, slave nor free, male nor female, for you are all one in Christ Jesus. [29]If you belong to Christ, then you are Abraham's seed, and heirs according to the promise. [4:1]What I am saying is that as long as the heir is a child, he is no different from a slave, although he owns the whole estate. [2]He is subject to guardians and trustees until the time set by his father. [3]So also, when we were children, we were in slavery under the basic principles of the world. [4]But when the time had fully come, God sent his Son, born of a woman, born under law, [5]to redeem those under law, that we might receive the full rights of sons. [6]Because you are sons, God sent the Spirit of his Son into our hearts, the Spirit who calls out, "Abba, Father." [7]So you are no longer a slave, but a son; and since you are a son, God has made you also an heir.[8]Formerly, when you did not know God, you were slaves to those who by nature are not gods. [9]But now that you know God—or rather are known by God—how is it that you are turning back to those weak and miserable principles? Do you wish to be enslaved by them all over again? [10]You are observing special days and months and seasons and years! [11]I fear for you, that somehow I have wasted my efforts on you." Galatians 3:26-4:11

5. Apostle Paul reminded them of their depth of his relationship with them. He reminds them of his devotion to them when he was first among them. From this standpoint of relationship and caring, he appealed to them to realize the debilitating effects that their Judaizers had on them. He writes with conviction that these Judaizers were not interested in their well being as he, Apostle Paul was.

    "I plead with you, brothers, become like me, for I became like you. You have done me no wrong. [13]As you know, it was because of an illness that I first preached the gospel to you. [14]Even though my illness was a trial to you, you did not treat me with contempt or scorn. Instead, you welcomed me as if I were an angel of God, as if I were Christ Jesus himself. [15]What has happened to all your joy? I can testify that, if you could have done so, you would have torn out your eyes and given them to me. [16]Have I now become your enemy by telling you the truth? [17]Those people are zealous to win you over, but for no good. What they want is to alienate you from us, so that you may be zealous for them. [18]It is fine to be zealous, provided the purpose is good, and to be so always and not just when I am with you. [19]My dear children, for whom I am again in the pains of childbirth until Christ is formed in you, [20]how I wish I could be with you now and change my tone, because I am perplexed about you!" Galatians 4:12-20

6. Apostle Paul then cemented the true revelation behind Abraham, Hagar, Sarah, and their two sons with the illustration that all Christian Believers are Children of freedom, and not bound in slavery to laws, rules, rituals and religious practices.

    "Tell me, you who want to be under the law, are you not

aware of what the law says? ²²For it is written that Abraham had two sons, one by the slave woman and the other by the free woman. ²³His son by the slave woman was born in the ordinary way; but his son by the free woman was born as the result of a promise. ²⁴These things may be taken figuratively, for the women represent two covenants. One covenant is from Mount Sinai and bears children who are to be slaves: This is Hagar. ²⁵Now Hagar stands for Mount Sinai in Arabia and corresponds to the present city of Jerusalem, because she is in slavery with her children. ²⁶But the Jerusalem that is above is free, and she is our mother. ²⁷For it is written: "Be glad, O barren woman, who bears no children; break forth and cry aloud, you who have no labour pains; because more are the children of the desolate woman than of her who has a husband." ²⁸Now you, brothers, like Isaac, are children of promise. ²⁹At that time the son born in the ordinary way persecuted the son born by the power of the Spirit. It is the same now. ³⁰But what does the Scripture say? "Get rid of the slave woman and her son, for the slave woman's son will never share in the inheritance with the free woman's son." ³¹Therefore, brothers, we are not children of the slave woman, but of the free woman." Galatians 4:21-31

7. Because the Judaizers were seeking to enforce physical circumcision as a necessity to salvation, Apostle Paul drives home the point that Jesus Christ sets us free, and rituals of man did not have any place in the life of the Believer. Therefore, Gentiles need not and should not be circumcised.

"It is for freedom that Christ has set us free. Stand firm, then, and do not let yourselves be burdened again by a yoke of slavery. ²Mark my words! I, Paul, tell you that if you let yourselves be circumcised, Christ will be of no value to you at all. ³Again I declare to every man who lets himself be circumcised that he is obligated to obey the whole law. ⁴You who are trying to be justified by law have been alienated from Christ; you have fallen away from grace. [5]But by faith we eagerly await through the Spirit the righteousness for which we hope. [6]For in Christ Jesus neither circumcision nor uncircumcision has any value. The only thing that counts is faith expressing itself through love. [7]You were running a good race. Who cut in on you and kept you from obeying the truth? [8]That kind of persuasion does not come from the one who calls you. [9]"A little yeast works through the whole batch of dough." [10]I am confident in the Lord that you will take no other view. The one who is throwing you into confusion will pay the penalty, whoever he may be. [11]Brothers, if I am still preaching circumcision, why am I still being persecuted? In that case the offense of the cross has been abolished. [12]As for those agitators, I wish they would go the whole way and emasculate themselves!" Galatians 5:1-12

The leaven of the Galatians was folly, legalism or salvation by works rather than trusting in the Grace of God. It also represents religiosity, walking in the flesh rather than the Spirit, being bewitched and turning away from "Present Truth[6]"!

This leaven is still prevalent in many circles of the Christian Church as the "Judaizers" type of Believer is still very much alive and active. Permit me to go a bit deeper in this letter that Apostle Paul wrote to the Galatians' church as it deals with so many issues that need to be dealt with today.

There are many who still hold the belief that an unsaved Jew is more righteous, holier, and more important to God and His Purpose than a Born-Again, Believer in Jesus Christ. Some Believers support everything that Israel does whether good and benevolent or evil and that all Jews regardless of their spiritual state will be saved. They **are** known as Zionists Christian but the downside of this belief system is that it has the added effect of turning Christian Zionists into supporters of Jewish Zionism which is politically based. They believe that the people of Israel as they are today [whether Born-Again or not] remain part of the Chosen

---

[6] For a more comprehensive understanding of "Present Truth" see the author's book – "Five Pillars of the Apostolic". Orderings details at the end of this book.

People of God, along with the engrafted Gentile Christians[7].

> "If some of the branches have been broken off, and you, though a wild olive shoot, have been grafted in among the others and now share in the nourishing sap from the olive root, [18]do not boast over those branches. If you do, consider this: You do not support the root, but the root supports you. [19]You will say then, "Branches were broken off so that I could be grafted in." [20]Granted. But they were broken off because of unbelief, and you stand by faith. Do not be arrogant, but be afraid. [21]For if God did not spare the natural branches, he will not spare you either. [22]*Consider therefore the kindness and sternness of God: sternness to those who fell*, but kindness to you, provided that you continue in his kindness. Otherwise, you also will be cut off. [23]*And if they do not persist in unbelief, they will be grafted in, for God is able to graft them in again.* [24]After all, if you were cut out of an olive tree that is wild by nature, and contrary to nature were grafted into a cultivated olive tree, how much more readily will these, the natural branches, be grafted into their own olive tree!" [Italics added] Romans 11:17-24

From this we see that the leaven that the Apostle Paul had to contend with in the Galatians' church was regarding the Jews seeking to inflict its customs and Jewish traditions and laws upon the True Church of Jesus Christ. We still have large sectors within the Church today that are still seeking to make the Church a Jewish religion and that is not right!

We need to understand that God is not Jewish, He is GOD! He existed long before there was even one human being upon the planet much less a race. We have to comprehend that God is not seeking to restore the Jewish race or religion, as this propels itself. It doesn't need to be re-established. First and foremost, God is wanting His Kingdom to be fully established in the earth. He wants all the kingdoms of this world to become the Kingdom of

---

[7] See also Dual-covenant theology.

our Lord and of His Christ. He wants every knee to bow and for every tongue to confess to the Lordship of His Son, Jesus Christ!

We have to understand that ultimately if Adam and Eve [who were not Jews] had not sinned we would not have had any division or sectors in the human race as we know it today. We need to fully grasp exactly what God had in mind when He first created Adam and Eve – a relationship of sweet fellowship with their God, and, that is still very much His agenda even today.

Apostle Paul went to the very heart of the issue that made the Jews separate to all other nations and that was circumcision. He revealed that circumcision was no longer a fleshly, earthy matter and what God was truly after was the circumcision of the heart.

The Jews boasted that Abraham was their father and thus were entitled to full birthrights. Then Apostle Paul took that opportunity by taking their rich lineage in the story of Abraham, Hagar, Sarah, and their two sons, and drawing parallels for the Jews with this story involving their forefathers in an allegory for all Christian Believers. Just as Isaac was the son of promise, those who confessed Jesus Christ in the Galatians' church were also the true Children of freedom, and not likened to the son of slavery, as was Ishmael.

Permit me to go a bit deeper in the argument from the allegory of Galatians 4:21-31 that was earlier referenced:

"For it is written, that Abraham had two sons, one by the bondwoman and one by the freewoman. But the son by the bondwoman was born according to the flesh, and the son by the freewoman through promise" [Galatians 4:22-23]. One son was born by the ordinary course of nature, the other by promise. According to nature, there was no reason to expect that Sarah should have a son.

> "This is allegorically speaking, for these women are two covenants; one proceeding from Mount Sinai, bearing children who are to be slaves; she is Hagar. [25]Now this Hagar is Mount Sinai in Arabia and corresponds to the present Jerusalem, for she is in slavery with her children.

²⁶But the Jerusalem that is above is free, she is our mother. ²⁷For it is written, Rejoice, barren woman who does not bear; break forth and shout, you who are not in labour; for more numerous are the children of the desolate than of the one who has a husband" [NJKV] Galatians 4:24-27.

Although used as an allegory for the purpose of illustration, these events were also literal and historical. Hagar represents the Mosaic Law and slavery. Sarah represents the promise given to Abraham. Mount Sinai represents Jerusalem in its present state under slavery to Rome, to the flesh and also it represents the Jews who adhere to the Law and continue in their infidelity and in their religious customs and bondage, hoping to please God.

Sarah and Isaac represent the Abrahamic Covenant. The Church is to be the Bride of Jesus Christ forever, represented by Sarah and Isaac [the Heavenly Jerusalem, the True Church, made up of all nations] and not Hagar and Ishmael [the earthly Jerusalem, the Jewish system, the Law].

In these verses, Apostle Paul illustrated the difference between Believers who rest in Jesus Christ only and Judaizers who trusted in the Law, by a comparison taken from the story of Isaac and Ishmael. This he introduced in such a manner as to get their attention by making an impression on their minds and by convincing them they were making a big mistake in falling away from the truth.

He takes it for granted that they did hear the Law, for among the Jews it was read in their public assemblies every Sabbath day. Since they were so very fond of being under the Law, Apostle Paul wanted them to know what was written in Genesis Chapters 1 and 21. His idea was, if they knew what was written in the two Chapters they might see how little reason they had to still trust in the Law.

We Born-Again Christians, who have accepted Jesus Christ, and rely upon Him, and look for justification and salvation by Him alone, we have become the spiritual seed of Abraham. Though we are not the natural seed of Abraham, by becoming the spiritual seed we are entitled to the promised inheritance.

To the Galatians who wavered in their faith in Jesus Christ and whose ears itched due to the gospel of the Judaizers which stressed obedience to ceremonial law under threats of persecution, the Apostle Paul arms them with the necessary tools to refute these false teachers. In Genesis 21:10-12 he tells the Galatians to radically "Cast out the bondservant and her son. For the son of the bondservant shall not be an heir with the son of free woman." Apostle Paul was attempting to show them that holdover Judaism would cause them to sink, wither, and perish; but true Christianity would flourish and last forever.

Apostle Paul emphatically concludes in his arguments that justification is by faith only and not a combination of faith and works. Those who advocate justification by faith and works are walking in darkness. Paul supports his claim with Scripture as he writes "we are not children of the bondwoman, but of the free" [Galatians 4:31].

As Believers we must guard against the leaven of the Galatians. Do you feel closer to God if you pray with a Jewish prayer shawl on your head? That can become a ritual. To onlookers it may appear more spiritual, and before long, everyone only prays with a prayer shawl on their heads. I use this illustration only to illustrate a point.

There is nothing inherently wrong with wearing a prayer shawl but if waves of ceremonial decorum become interwoven with faith, and you cannot pray because you left your shawl at home, this becomes the beginning of religious leaven. Leaven of this sort must be eradicated from the ranks of professing Christianity if we are to see the Church come into a place of maturity!

CHAPTER 7

THE LEAVEN OF HEROD

We are most familiar with the leaven of the Pharisees with its' corrupting influence whenever the word "leaven" is mentioned but Mark 8:15 mentions another type of leaven, one that may be unfamiliar to you:

> "Then He charged them, saying, "Take heed, beware of the leaven of the Pharisees and the leaven of Herod." Mark 8:15

The leaven of Herod is not usually a separate subject of study or discussion when referencing the effect of leaven as usually they get lumped together – the leaven of the Pharisees and the leaven of Herod. But we do well to explore the impact of this statement. Herod was the tetrarch of Galilee, the son of Herod the Great and he contributed greatly to the corrupt leaven weaving its way into Jewish society.

Under the Roman system of government the territory of Galilee was under the joint rule of four rulers. Herod like his father before him, was ruthless in his rule and interestingly enough, he was the only monarch who reigned with a watered-down lineage. He was Jewish only on his father's side and the lineage of his mother was that of a Samaritan. This in itself placed Herod in a negative light as the Samaritans were despised by ordinary Jews. A Jew believed that he could become contaminated by passing through Samaritan territory, and therefore would detour to avoid such a trek.

Likewise, the Samaritans often taunted the Jews. They rejected all of the Old Testament except the Pentateuch, and they claimed to have an older copy of the Book, therefore a more precise guidebook which allowed them to boast that they could observe the precepts better. According to John 4:12, the Jews repaid the Samaritans with hatred. They rejected the Samaritan copy of the Law and publicly denounced that Samaritans were of any Jewish birth [John 4:12].

Herod fought a battle within himself and in a time where power and position were in direct alignment with keeping the bloodlines pure, Herod had to show his strength and power by keeping his subjects at bay. This was certainly evident in the corruption of his rule from these glimpses into his life from Scripture.

Rule in the Roman system was usually achieved by those who gained [by bribes, or service] the favour of Caesar. The whole system was corrupt. It was not the office of the king that was corrupt in and of itself; but rather the warnings of Jesus Christ about the leaven of Herod, pointed to the process of gaining this office which was corrupt as it could be gotten by bribes. It had a strong influence on Israel as a society, without thought of integrity or transparency.

[8]As far as the Herodians were concerned, nothing was actually sinful; and as long as you 'believed' in God, everything was okay. In fact, according to historians, the Herodians were an influential religious and political group comprised of Jews who catered to Herod, accepted the Roman way of life, and were favourable toward Greek customs and passions. In other words, these were the supposedly 'enlightened' Jews who claimed they had faith in God, yet curried political and social favour by not imposing their beliefs on others. The Herodians were the *"inclusive church"*, the *"politically correct church"*, and indeed the *"cool church"* of their day.

In their own demented way, the Herodians actually thought that by embracing the world's system and values and incorporating them into their Jewish 'faith', they could not only draw more followers into their 'denomination', but be able to preserve it as well. This colossal deception led to the Herodians becoming the ultimate

---

[8] From Larry Ocasio of Other Side Ministries – www.othersideministries.com

compromisers. As a result, rather than being a force for good in their communities they fostered a culture of perverse laws and ungodly practices, and these self-centred man-pleasers instead became agents of and to the anti-Christ spirit.

Today, in their desire to make God's Word more "socially acceptable" many so-called ministers are presenting a form of '*Herodianism*' under the guise of Christianity. For instance, in a current movement known as the "Emergent Church", many of its leaders are now questioning the timeless and fundamental doctrines of our Christian faith. Doctrines such as the reality of hell, the call to holiness, and the Deity of Jesus Christ just to name a few. In his book the "Velvet Elvis", Emergent Church leader Rob Bell presents the case that if we get rid of the antiquated doctrine of the virgin birth we really don't lose anything at all! According to Mr. Bell, finding out that Jesus Christ was born naturally rather than *super*-naturally "shouldn't change our view of God." Staying true to form, these modern-day Herodian leaders also refuse to address sin, while proclaiming a gospel of 'grace' that denies the need for repentance. Like their predecessors, these self-centred man-pleasers seek only to increase their numbers by promoting a hedonistic, non-judgmental worldview rather than a Christ-centred Biblical one. They shamefully and inaccurately present Jesus as an all-inclusive god who has no boundaries, no distinct form of holiness and no absolute truth.

Having said that, the "Emergent church" is not alone; several denominations in their quest to make the gospel more "culturally connective" are not only marrying homosexual couples but also promoting them into leadership positions. Not to be outdone, many Charismatic church leaders are now embracing "New Age" philosophies such as using visualization techniques in order to attain 'spiritual' climaxes, while at the same time, exalting 'angelic' and supposedly 'prophetic' experiences above the written Word of God. All this combined with the countless unsanctified teachings on God's grace have served to create a contemporary Christian environment where fewer and fewer people can discern right from wrong or the holy from the profane.

In fact, this Herodian spirit has infiltrated the church to such an extent that millions of church-going folks now actually think that abortion is *"okay"*, that maybe the Jews *"are"* to blame for the ills of the world, and that Jesus Christ isn't necessarily the *"only"* way to heaven. Like the Herodians of old, many so-called 'believers' have embraced the world's political and moral perspective while still claiming to follow Jesus Christ. This is the height of deception!

This is no small thing we are dealing with. While today's Herodian preachers may be more sophisticated and nuanced, their demonically inspired intent is still the same: to destroy the testimony of Jesus Christ! The strategy for doing so has also not changed, you just have to compromise your beliefs and make the Gospel more culturally 'relevant' by moving away from the absolute and eternal doctrines that anchor our faith. However, we must understand that whenever we pervert the beauty and sanctity of God's Word in order to gain acceptance by the world, we become defiled and abhorred lovers who are quickly discarded once our usefulness has ended.

"When the Church lowers her testimony for God to the carnal tastes of the world, with a view to conciliation, she loses everything and gains nothing." — Jamieson-Faust-Brown

We can never increase God's Kingdom by lowering His standards or by creating doctrines of demons. How foolish to assume that God's Will can be produced by *changing* His Word.

The only defence against the leaven of Herod is truth. The uncompromised Word of God, spoken through pure and uncompromised vessels is what changed the world in the First Century and it is what will change our world today. John the Baptist, in the midst of a wicked king and culture stood boldly and courageously on God's Word even at the cost of his own life. You and I must do likewise. We must unashamedly present these truths with the love of God, while aggressively and steadfastly opposing anything and anyone that tries to turn the grace of God into the leaven of Herod. [7]

John the Baptist and Herod:

"King Herod heard about this, for Jesus' name had become well known. Some were saying, "John the Baptist has been raised from the dead, and that is why miraculous powers are at work in him." [15]Others said, "He is Elijah." And still others claimed, "He is a prophet, like one of the prophets of long ago." [16]But when Herod heard this, he said, "John, the man I beheaded, has been raised from the dead!" [17]For Herod himself had given orders to have John arrested, and he had him bound and put in prison. He did this because of Herodias, his brother Philip's wife, whom he had married. [18]For John had been saying to Herod, "It is not lawful for you to have your brother's wife." [19]So Herodias nursed a grudge against John and wanted to kill him. But she was not able to, [20]because Herod feared John and protected him, knowing him to be a righteous and holy man. When Herod heard John, he was greatly puzzled; yet he liked to listen to him. [21]Finally the opportune time came. On his birthday Herod gave a banquet for his high officials and military commanders and the leading men of Galilee. [22]When the daughter of Herodias came in and danced, she pleased Herod and his dinner guests. The king said to the girl, "Ask me for anything you want, and I'll give it to you." [23]And he promised her with an oath, "Whatever you ask I will give you, up to half my kingdom." [24]She went out and said to her mother, "What shall I ask for?" "The head of John the Baptist," she answered. [25]At once the girl hurried in to the king with the request: "I want you to give me right now the head of John the Baptist on a platter." [26]The king was greatly distressed, but because of his oaths and his dinner guests, he did not want to refuse her. [27]So he immediately sent an executioner with orders to bring John's head. The man went, beheaded John in the prison, [28]and brought back his head on a platter. He presented it to the girl, and she gave it to her mother. [29]On hearing of this, John's disciples came and took his body and laid it in a tomb."
Mark 6:14-29

The above passage of Scripture reveals that Herod was the one who gave the orders to murder John the Baptist. Scripture also reveals that John the Baptist came in the spirit and power of Elijah. In Elijah's time he had to deal with this same political spirit that sought to have total domination and control over the Children of Israel. This spirit which appeared on scene in the form of Jezebel, the arch-rival who tried to destroy Elijah. Permit me to unmask the spirit of [9]Jezebel before continuing:

The Jezebel Spirit:
The name Jezebel means – "un-co-habited". The woman sporting this name was very much married. So in essence Jezebel means "one who is uncovered or one who will not submit to authority". Although we are considering this woman's name and what it means, please understand that this is not a woman or even a gender thing; it is a spirit that affects both male and female. It is an unclean spirit that seeks to manipulate and control governmental authority or leadership within the Church, and can only function effectively whenever there is weak leadership as exemplified in Jezebel's husband Ahab.

> "But there was no one like Ahab who sold himself to do wickedness in the sight of the LORD, *because Jezebel his wife stirred him up*. [26]And he behaved very abominably in following idols, according to all that the Amorites had done, whom the LORD had cast out before the children of Israel." [Italics added NJKV] 1 Kings 21:25-26

Jezebel's entry into Israel was through the gateway of marriage[10]. As a matter of fact Ahab married Jezebel in total contradiction to the law laid down by God, which states:

> "When the LORD your God brings you into the land which you go to possess, and has cast out many nations before you, the Hittites and the Girgashites and the Amorites and the Canaanites and the Perizzites and the

<hr>

[9] See the author's book titled "Identifying and Defeating the Jezebel Spirit" – ordering details at the end of this book.
[10] 1 Kings 16:29-31

Hivites and the Jebusites, seven nations greater and mightier than you, ²and when the LORD your God delivers them over to you, you shall conquer them and utterly destroy them. You shall make no covenant with them nor show mercy to them. ³*Nor shall you make marriages with them*. You shall not give your daughter to their son, nor take their daughter for your son. ⁴For they will turn your sons away from following Me, to serve other gods; so the anger of the LORD will be aroused against you and destroy you suddenly." [Italics added NJKV] Deuteronomy 7:1-4

After entering illegally, she established a false system of government, by having ¹¹four hundred and fifty prophets personally serve her in her evil ways. Jezebel attacked and ¹²massacred the legitimate, God-ordained authority of her day. The Jezebel spirit continues to exist even today and attacks true, legitimate, God-ordained, ministry – ministry that has vision and that can discern the heart and mind of God. She represents a bold, demonic authority that wants to kill legitimate, God-ordained ministry and she does not want any form of retaliation.

The following passage of Scripture reveals the true nature and foundation of the spirit of Jezebel:

"And it came to pass after these things that Naboth the Jezreelite had a vineyard which was in Jezreel, next to the palace of Ahab king of Samaria. ²So Ahab spoke to Naboth, saying, "Give me your vineyard, that I may have it for a vegetable garden, because it is near, next to my house; and for it I will give you a vineyard better than it. Or, if it seems good to you, I will give you its worth in money." ³*But Naboth said to Ahab, "The LORD forbid that I should give the inheritance of my fathers to you!"* ⁴So Ahab went into his house sullen and displeased because of the word which Naboth the Jezreelite had spoken to him; for he had said, "I will not give you the

---

¹¹ 1 Kings 18:19
¹² 1 Kings 18:4

inheritance of my fathers." And he lay down on his bed, and turned away his face, and would eat no food. [5]But Jezebel his wife came to him, and said to him, "Why is your spirit so sullen that you eat no food?" [6]He said to her, "Because I spoke to Naboth the Jezreelite, and said to him, 'Give me your vineyard for money; or else, if it pleases you, I will give you another vineyard for it.' And he answered, 'I will not give you my vineyard.' [7]"Then *Jezebel his wife said to him, "You now exercise authority over Israel! Arise, eat food, and let your heart be cheerful; I will give you the vineyard of Naboth the Jezreelite."* [8]*And she wrote letters in Ahab's name, sealed them with his seal,* and sent the letters to the elders and the nobles who were dwelling in the city with Naboth. [9]She wrote in the letters, saying, Proclaim a fast, and seat Naboth with high honour among the people; [10]and seat two men, scoundrels, before him to bear witness against him, saying, "You have blasphemed God and the king." Then take him out, and stone him, that he may die. [11]So the men of his city, the elders and nobles who were inhabitants of his city, did as Jezebel had sent to them, as it was written in the letters, which she had sent to them. [12]They proclaimed a fast, and seated Naboth with high honour among the people. [13]And two men, scoundrels, came in and sat before him; and the scoundrels witnessed against him, against Naboth, in the presence of the people, saying, "Naboth has blasphemed God and the king!" [14]Then they took him outside the city and stoned him with stones, so that he died. Then they sent to Jezebel, saying, "Naboth has been stoned and is dead." [15]And it came to pass, *when Jezebel heard that Naboth had been stoned and was dead, that Jezebel said to Ahab, "Arise, take possession of the vineyard of Naboth the Jezreelite, which he refused to give you for money; for Naboth is not alive, but dead."* [16]So it was, when Ahab heard that Naboth was dead, that Ahab got up and went down to take possession of the vineyard of Naboth the Jezreelite." [Italics added NKJV] 1 Kings 21:1-16

Points To Extract from the study of Jezebel:

- She married into weak leadership.

- She sought to manipulate and control leadership.

- She usurped authority to conduct evil.

- She was seemingly a loving wife who was willing to get her husband anything he wanted – a false display of loyalty.

And she was not simply an Old Testament travesty but a power to be reckoned with even today as the *Lord warned us of this spirit* entering the New Testament Church.

> "Nevertheless I have a few things against you, because you allow *that woman Jezebel, who calls herself a prophetess, to teach and seduce* My servants to commit sexual immorality and eat things sacrificed to idols." [Italics added] Revelation 2:20

The spirit of Jezebel disguises itself in the prophetic realm where it rises up in an attempt to bring revelation to the Church by means of teaching. But in direct opposition to the true Elijah anointing and spirit of the last days, this false prophetess brings a [13]counterfeit of the true Apostolic ministry being restored in the last days.

She uses seduction as her main tactic. Seduction is a cunning, well-planned system of attack with the sole intent of misleading and deceiving.

Further Dynamics Of The Jezebel Spirit:
The Jezebel spirit attains importance in the Church through legitimate alliance with leadership.

Ahab, then king over Israel in an attempt to forge stronger political or leadership ties with the king of Tyre/Sidon, married the then king's daughter.

In the days of David and Solomon a beneficial commercial inter-

---

[13] 2 Corinthians 11:13-15

course existed between the Hebrews and the Phoenicians. Ahab, recognizing the advantages that his kingdom would accrue from an alliance with the foremost commercial nation of his time, renewed the old relations with the Phoenicians and cemented them by his marriage with Jezebel, daughter of Ethbaal, king of Tyre.

Ahab strengthened the friendly relations with Phoenicia that David had begun when he was king of the United Kingdom. He sealed the friendship between the two nations with a political marriage to Jezebel, the notoriously wicked daughter of Ethbaal, king of the Sidonians [1 Kings 16:31]. Ahab was the first king of Israel to establish peaceful relations with Judah.

When not in tune with the Holy Spirit, these alliances, although not God-ordained and therefore evil, will be hailed and accommodated by the Church as necessary for growth and increase. Remember, the Lord already warned us about this in the Book of Revelation Chapter 2 and verse 20, as was previously alluded to. The Jezebel spirit is permitted to teach, a function that is necessary for healthy Church growth and Christian maturity.

The spirit of Jezebel can manifest through highly capable and gifted persons who through legitimate alliance, hold keys to policy and influence over decisions.

This spirit loves to work from within leadership, Jezebel deflects worship from God – to an "Owner," "Master," "Husband," or "Father" whose permissiveness allows idolatry and sexual looseness that accelerates with time.

The influence of the Jezebel spirit is particularly evident in her absence. Innocence, a renewed desire to please God, a dependence on Him and contriteness, however short-lived, will be seen when Jezebel leaves Ahab's side.

Rebellion among the Body of Believers will be rampant and the impenitent will be plagued by practices of the occult and of witchcraft. Conviction will wane within the Church Body as obduracy will prevent repentance.

Her death is marked with the death of the entire dynasty or leadership that have had dealings with, or supported her. But even in the face of collapse, she will use her wiles and accusations on chosen servants to buy time to regain her footing. Beware!

Jesus Christ's Encounter with the Leaven of Herod:

"Now it happened that He went through the grainfields on the Sabbath; and as they went His disciples began to pluck the heads of grain. [24]And the Pharisees said to Him, "Look, why do they do what is not lawful on the Sabbath?" [25]But He said to them, "Have you never read what David did when he was in need and hungry, he and those with him: [26]how he went into the house of God in the days of Abiathar the high priest, and ate the showbread, which is not lawful to eat, except for the priests, and also gave some to those who were with him?" [27]And He said to them, "The Sabbath was made for man, and not man for the Sabbath. [28]Therefore the Son of Man is also Lord of the Sabbath. [3:1]And He entered the synagogue again, and a man was there who had a withered hand. [2]So they watched Him closely, whether He would heal him on the Sabbath, so that they might accuse Him. [3]And He said to the man who had the withered hand, "Step forward." [4]Then He said to them, "Is it lawful on the Sabbath to do good or to do evil, to save life or to kill?" But they kept silent. [5]And when He had looked around at them with anger, being grieved by the hardness of their hearts, He said to the man, "Stretch out your hand." And he stretched it out, and his hand was restored as whole as the other. [6]Then the Pharisees went out and immediately plotted with the Herodians against Him, how they might destroy Him". Mark 2: 23-3:6

"Then the Pharisees went and plotted how they might entangle Him in His talk. [16]And they sent to Him their disciples with the Herodians, saying, "Teacher, we know that You are true, and teach the way of God in truth; nor do You care about anyone, for You do not regard the person of men. [17]Tell us, therefore, what do You think? Is it lawful to pay taxes to Caesar, or not?" [18]But Jesus perceived their wickedness, and said, "Why do you test Me, you hypocrites? [19]Show Me the tax money." So they brought Him a denarius. [20]And He said to them, "Whose image and inscription is this?" [21]They said to Him, "Caesar's." And He said to them, "Render therefore to Caesar the things that are Caesar's, and to God the things that are God's." [22]When they had heard these words, they marvelled, and left Him and went their way." Matthew 22:15-22

The leaven of Herod is malice, deceit and political guile – Herod used his political office to enforce his way and the Jews played up to his system to get rid of Jesus Christ. He sharply warned of the destruction wrought by religious politics in the Church – Church politics manifest when we seek to try and manipulate and gain control by using people. This also happens when people begin to play up to men by seeking to gain an advantage for their own selfish and sometimes evil end. For example in some churches through a voting process mixed with manipulation they rid themselves of Senior Leaders or anyone they do not like. It is sad when the *leaven of Herod* enters a church or ministry.

Earthly politics within the Church is one the most deceptive and dangerous realms that need to be effectively dealt with. Allow me to go a bit deeper with this particular dimension:

Politics – Webster's Dictionary Definition:
Wise; prudent and sagacious in devising and pursuing measures adapted to promote the public welfare; applied to persons.

Well devised and adapted to the public prosperity.
Ingenious in devising and pursuing any scheme of personal or national enhancement, without regard to the morality of the measure; cunning; artful; sagacious in adapting means to the end, whether good or evil...

Well devised; adapted to its end, right or wrong.

1. The art or science of government or the art or science concerned with guiding or influencing governmental policy.

2. Political affairs or business; *especially*: competition between competing interest groups or individuals for power and leadership [as in a government].

    ▪ Political life especially as a principal activity or profession.

    ▪ Political activities characterized by artful and often dishonest practices.

3. The total complex of relations between people living in society; b: relations or conduct in a particular area of experience especially as seen or dealt with from a political point of view such as: "office *politics*" or "ethnic *politics*".

Political – Pertaining to *policy*, or to civil government and its administration. Political measures or affairs are measures that respect the government of a nation or state.

Policy – from which the word police is derived:

1. Prudence or wisdom in the management of affairs.

    ▪ Management or procedure based primarily on material interest.

2. A definite course or method of action selected from among alternatives and in light of given conditions to guide and determine present and future decisions.

    ▪ A high-level overall plan embracing the general goals and acceptable procedures especially of a governmental body.

In earthly Politics there is the Government and then there is the Opposition, whose task it is, to oppose the ruling Government and to seek to dig up as much dirt on the other party as is possible.

We hear politicians who with fervour declare: "my job is to oppose the Government", and rightly or wrongly they do so, as they see it as their job. The results do not matter, they simply oppose. It is as though being in agreement evokes some form of weakness, or lack of political prowess. Fools will evoke the same results if they cannot see the side of reason. As such we cannot afford that spirit to enter the Church, where certain members feel it is their duty or responsibility to oppose any and everything put forward by the leaders.

Interestingly, a survey done by Ipsos-Reid for Sympatico.MSN.ca to find out which professionals do Canadians trust the most? Here are some of their findings listed as: *The Trust Factor*

Percentage of Canadians who felt they could trust someone according to profession:

1. *Firefighters 93*
2. Nurses 87
3. Pharmacists 86
4. Airline pilots 81
5. Doctors 80
6. *Police officers 69*
7. *Teachers 69*
8. Armed forces personnel 65
9. Daycare workers 61
10. Accountants 54
11. Judges 52
12. Chiropractors 49
13. Financial advisers 47
14. Employees of charities 41
15. Environmentalists 39
16. Plumbers 39
17. *Religious workers 37*
18. Judicial system workers 33
19. TV/Radio personalities 29
20. Real estate agents 28
21. Journalists 26
22. Lawyers 25
23. Auto mechanics 25
24. New home builders 23
25. Members of the press 23

Church Politics/Politicians:
Sad to say that this spirit is abiding [as a matter of fact; has been invited] into some churches and ministries. I believe with that the Lord desires that we be proactive and pre-empt this spirit from making any attempts to hijack the Church.

Allow me to categorically state, that the Government of God and the government of the earth are definitely two different operations. And what has happened is that the Church a lot of times models its Government after the order of the earth! By doing this we are opening the doors for the Leaven of Herod to gain its foothold!

Immunization Or Inoculation:
As I awoke early one morning the Lord began speaking to me about the power of *inoculations* and gave me the imagery of young children and how they are inoculated against certain known diseases as a preventative measure.

Among all the medical advances of the past two centuries, immunization or inoculation has contributed greatly to improved health and increased life expectancy. It provides the best possible protection against some very serious known diseases. And in like manner we can do the same in our churches. We need to inoculate ourselves against the very things that seek to destroy the True Church. We need to be proactive and war against the very things that seek to destroy us!

Hear me *Church Politics* is a known disease that cripples the immune system of the *Body*! That's why we need Watchmen on our Walls; the inoculation provided for us. Remember that in Israel they had Watchmen on the Walls of Jerusalem. The Lord then spoke to me that as Watchmen we are to be watching for two things:

1. We are to watch as wise Virgins being prepared to look for the Lord's Coming – the Moves of The Holy Spirit in revealing Jesus Christ to His Church and extending His Kingdom rule in nations.

2. We are to watch for movements of the enemy as he seeks to thwart the forward advance of God's Kingdom and Church in the earth. In so doing we pre-empt or circumvent his attacks and manoeuvres. After all, sometimes the best war is the one that did not happen.

While in prayer one morning the Lord said to me that He was giving us Divine Intelligence and that we needed to be truly watchful. And as He reveals things to us that we should war and pre-empt some of them.

In order to thwart any attempt by the enemy to inflict the spirit of worldly politics upon the Church I believe one of our greatest weapons is that we must celebrate our differences! I believe that by celebrating our differences we would thereby be maximizing our strengths. We should celebrate our differences and use them for the benefit of the Body which would promote unity. Where there is unity, the Spirit of God moves. We should be nothing like earthly politicians where discord is rampant.

No man is an island, no congregation of the True Church becomes a law unto themselves, and none of us has some unique, special, or secret access to the Father. We are all needed and are necessary and if we could put our differences aside, it would leave no room for the leaven of Herod and the Government of the Lord Jesus Christ would truly begin to function as it was meant to function.

CHAPTER 8

THE LEAVEN OF THE CORINTHIANS

I n order to fully understand the leaven of the Corinthians, it would be very beneficial if we first understand a bit about the city and its origins.

[14]Corinth, or Korinth [Κόρινθος] is a Greek city, on the Isthmus of Corinth, the original Isthmus, the narrow stretch of land that joins the Peloponnesus to the mainland of Greece. To the west of the isthmus lies the Gulf of Corinth. Like its ancient predecessor, modern Corinth is the center of commerce between northern and southern Greece. Today, it has a population of about 30,000, far less than the estimated 500,000 in the days that Apostle Paul lived and ministered there.

Corinth is about 48 miles [78 km] west of Athens. The Isthmus, which was in ancient times traversed by hauling ships over the rocky ridge on sledges, is now cut by a canal. It is also the capital of the prefecture of Corinthia. The city is surrounded by Lechaio, Kalamaki, Loutraki, the Geraneia mountains, and the southern mountains.

The Corinth of Apostle Paul's day was relatively new. The old Corinth [which was famous and powerful in the days of the Peloponnesian War] was burned in 146 B.C. by the Roman proconsul, L. Mummius. Because it was a city devoted to the gods, a hundred years were required to pass before the city could be rebuilt. In 46 B.C., Julius Caesar rebuilt the city, populated it with a colony of veterans and free men, and named it Julia Corinthus.

---

[14] Adapted from an article at http://www.mlahanas.de/Greece/Regions/Geraneia.html

And soon, it became a very important commercial center.

With its new found reputation as being a prominent center of commerce in the Mediterranean world, it swiftly became a place for all sorts of vice. An example of its immorality was found in the temple of Venus [Aphrodite], which hosted 1000 priestesses dedicated to prostitution in the name of religion. The city became so well known for such immorality that the very name was made into a verb. To "corinthianize" literally meant to go to bed with a prostitute.

No doubt, the city's close proximity to the city of Athens probably added the problem of intellectualism. The Greeks had made discoveries in a wide spread of fields, most notably mathematics [Pythagoras], geometry [Euclid], astronomy [Ptolemy], science [Archimedes] and natural history [Aristotle]. Noted for their oratory skills, their philosophy and their architecture, Greek literature was treasured by the Romans and one can surmise that these works of Sophocles, Euripides, Herodotus, and Homer the poet were very much the centre of discussion in the marketplace. Environment wholeheartedly affects a people, perhaps more than we care to admit. And as we see in the epistle, such an environment had its effect upon the church in Corinth. It is amazing that a church existed at all in such a city.

The Corinthian church was made up of a core of Jewish Believers but many of its members were saved out of this pagan background, bringing with them their pagan practices in the newly established church. Apostle Paul arrived in Corinth in AD 51 to preach the Word of God. While there he established a church and remained in the church for 18 months to bring the Word of God to them [Acts 18:1-18]. A couple of years after leaving he received a letter from the church that explained some problems the church was having and asked for guidance [1 Corinthians 7:1]. He also received some additional information from an independent family [Chloe's household] in the church that further explained the problems the church was facing [1 Corinthians 1:11].

While the actual reference to leaven is found in the following passage of Scripture, its debilitating effects are plastered throughout the Apostle Paul's letter to the Corinthian Saints.

> "It is actually reported that there is *sexual immorality* among you, and such *sexual immorality* as is not even named among the Gentiles--that a man has his father's wife! ²And you are puffed up, and have not rather mourned, that he who has done this deed might be taken away from among you. ³For I indeed, as absent in body but present in spirit, have already judged (as though I were present) him who has so done this deed. ⁴In the name of our Lord Jesus Christ, when you are gathered together, along with my spirit, with the power of our Lord Jesus Christ, ⁵deliver such a one to Satan for the destruction of the flesh, that his spirit may be saved in the day of the Lord Jesus. ⁶Your glorying is not good. Do you not know that a little leaven leavens the whole lump? ⁷Therefore purge out the old leaven, that you may be a new lump, since you truly are unleavened. For indeed Christ, our Passover, was sacrificed for us. ⁸Therefore let us keep the feast, not with old leaven, nor with *the leaven of malice and wickedness*, but with the unleavened bread of sincerity and truth." [Italics added] 1 Corinthians 5:1-8

In this passage Apostle Paul makes it abundantly clear that the leaven he was referring to was sexual immorality, malice and wickedness. However, as one reads through this first letter to the Corinthians one cannot help but realize that there were many other problems that surfaced in the church. All of which was as the result of evil leaven manifesting itself.

One of the Corinthians' foundational problems was their inability to discern the work of the Holy Spirit. They didn't know what was of God and what wasn't. They were confusing the work of the Holy Spirit with pagan ecstasies – familiar holdovers from the former way of life of many of them. Old habits often die hard deaths and this was true of the Corinthian church.

As was referenced earlier on, the city of Corinth was founded on familiar pagan concepts and rituals. The Corinthians possessed the "if it feels good then do it" mentality. Many of them were now speaking in other tongues and believed that their experience was genuine Holy Ghost induced activity because it made them "feel good". Speaking in tongues by the power of the Holy Ghost has nothing to do with the "if it feels good do it" mentality. It is a baptism of power from on high and it comes as a result of the Believer seeking for more of God. It is all about Him, not a good time in another dimension. Let me hasten and say this – if we believe that experience supersedes the Word of God, then there is no way to authenticate the experience. As such they were indeed confusing the work of the Holy Spirit with pagan ecstasies and causing that influence [leaven] to enter the church with its attending corrupting influences.

Hence the reason Apostle Paul had to preface his teaching to them on the Gifts of The Holy Spirit; here is what he wrote:

> "Now *about spiritual gifts, brothers, I do not want you to be ignorant.* ²You know that *when you were pagans, somehow or other you were influenced and led astray to mute idols.* ³Therefore I tell you that *no one who is speaking by the Spirit of God says, "Jesus be cursed,"* and no one can say, "Jesus is Lord," except by the Holy Spirit." [Italics added] 1 Corinthians 12:1-3

> "Now *concerning spiritual gifts, brethren, I do not want you to be ignorant:* ²You know that *you were Gentiles, carried away to these dumb idols, however you were led.* ³Therefore I make known to you that *no one speaking by the Spirit of God calls Jesus accursed,* and no one can say that Jesus is Lord except by the Holy Spirit." [Italics added NKJV]

We will expound on several points of note here, as I believe that the leaven of the Corinthians is having its influence in the Church world even today:

Apostle Paul encouraged and warned them as a loving father. He didn't want them to be ignorant about the work of the Holy Spirit by pointing out that they were manifesting some ignorant behaviour. Please, understand that not all manifestations that we encounter in the Church today are of God.

He saw that they were being "carried away" in their newfound faith, to the point where their past pagan practices infiltrated their worship. Apparently, some of these old patterns of worship had surfaced in the church. In verse three the Apostle Paul writes – "Therefore I make known to you that *no one speaking by the Spirit of God calls Jesus accursed...*" There must have been some kind of bizarre manifestation or defamatory statements about Christ for Paul to be prompted to make such a statement. In essence it would suggest to us that some who were supposedly manifesting the gifts of the Holy Spirit, were actually saying, "Jesus be damned" – [maybe this was revealed through the interpretation of the tongues that some were speaking in]!

Evidently the Corinthian church members were in such a state of confusion, that they were unable to distinguish between what was of the Holy Spirit and what was of the flesh and demons. Sad to say, there are many today in that same pitiful spiritual condition. We need to ask ourselves if some of the behaviour [such as fainting, trances, angelic visitation, gold dust, feathers falling over the meeting, frenzied behaviour, or the ever popular being slain in the Spirit, etc] we witness happening today in many churches, is of God and if they can be substantiated by the New Testament of God's Word! The leaven of the Corinthians is still with us today and as such the warning given by the Holy Spirit through the Apostle Paul to the Corinthian church is still as valid as it was back then – we must stand against the permeation of the leaven of the Corinthians!!!

Remember that lucifer, the "fallen angel" masquerades as an angel of light and thereby has and still is deceiving many. The Apostle Paul stated it fiercely in his stinging defence of his Apostolic Call and function to the church at Corinth:

> "I am jealous for you with a godly jealousy. I promised you to one husband, to Christ, so that I might present you

as a pure virgin to him. [3]But I am afraid that just as Eve was deceived by the serpent's cunning, your minds may somehow be led astray from your sincere and pure devotion to Christ. [4]For if someone comes to you and preaches a Jesus other than the Jesus we preached, or if you receive a different spirit from the one you received, or a different gospel from the one you accepted, you put up with it easily enough. [5]But I do not think I am in the least inferior to those "super-apostles." ...[13]For such men are false apostles, deceitful workmen, masquerading as apostles of Christ. [14]*And no wonder, for satan himself masquerades as an angel of light.* [15]It is not surprising, then, if his servants masquerade as servants of righteousness. Their end will be what their actions deserve." [Italics added] 2 Corinthians 11:2-5, 13-15

Angels have become objects of worship, as leaders in an attempt to fleece the people of God are always talking about angels and how they were able to see and talk to these angels and that the angel told them to do such and such. After the crowd is mesmerized by this "angel talk", they leave the meetings with their pockets turned inside out as they are called to give special offerings to garner the blessings of the angels when in those states of stupor.

I have even heard of meetings where Christians who allegedly come under the influence of the Holy Spirit start making animal noises such as roaring like a lion or barking like a dog all in the Name of the power of the Holy Ghost. There have been other bizarre manifestations – people who shake and quake and fall down and convulse; some even crow like roosters all in the name of revival and freedom in the "spirit"... Where in God's Word do we find such manifestations being called filled with the Holy Spirit or "freedom in the Spirit"? Nowhere!

I could understand these manifestations happening in a meeting where people are being delivered from unclean spirits as these types of manifestations occurred in the Word of God. Let me cite a few examples:

"When Jesus saw that a crowd was running to the scene, he rebuked the evil spirit. "You deaf and mute spirit," he said, "I command you, come out of him and never enter him again." 26The spirit shrieked, convulsed him violently and came out. The boy looked so much like a corpse that many said, "He's dead." 27But Jesus took him by the hand and lifted him to his feet, and he stood up." Mark 9:25-27

"They went into Capernaum; and immediately on the Sabbath He entered the synagogue and began to teach. 22They were amazed at His teaching; for He was teaching them as one having authority, and not as the scribes. 23Just then there was a man in their synagogue with an unclean spirit; and he cried out, 24saying, "What business do we have with each other, Jesus of Nazareth? Have You come to destroy us? I know who You are–the Holy One of God!" 25And Jesus rebuked him, saying, "Be quiet, and come out of him!" 26Throwing him into convulsions, the unclean spirit cried out with a loud voice and came out of him." [NASB] Mark 1:21-26

For Believers caught up in such activities and actions, it is a shameful thing, but it presents a much deeper problem among the leadership positions in the Body of Christ! I say this because a lot of these behaviours are sometimes televised globally and when some of the false teachers and preachers of such error come crashing down and are exposed for who they really are, there is no global rebuke and calling the error for what it is! Instead these leaders are scooped up by their peers and revived only to continue in their deception! Leaders must be held to a higher standard – period!

Again the Apostle John strongly warned the early Church and even more so today's Believers"

"Dear friends, do not believe every spirit, but test the spirits to see whether they are from God, because many false prophets have gone out into the world." 1 John 4:1

"My dear friends, don't believe everything you hear. Carefully weigh and examine what people tell you. Not everyone who talks about God comes from God. There are a lot of lying preachers loose in the world." [MSG]

Being Slain in the Spirit or Falling Down Under the Power of God:

This is another phenomenon that we have to examine very closely as this a very legitimate experience. Many of the patriarchs experienced this, and members of the early Church experienced it, especially the Apostles. However, there are some things that we need to examine so that we can establish the genuine from the false.

In Scripture whenever someone falls down under the power of God it is never without some level of understanding.

Today there are so many who "fall under the power of God" but they often do so without any knowledge as to the reason for this occurrence. The person being prayed for falls and they are completely out of it and another person in the prayer line sees others falling and decides [perhaps subconsciously] that it is the thing to do. Some fall because they are pushed down by some over exuberant preachers. While it is understandable that when folks are pushed down they have no other choice but to fall backwards, Scripture does not have one occurrence in the New Testament where a Believer or even in the Old Testament where the people of God fell down backwards at the Presence of the Lord, either by His Spirit or from the presence of one of His Angels.

Some expositors have noted that in all Biblical instances of the powerful Presence of God causing one to fall prostrate, the position was always face down while in contemporary instances, the worshipper falls backward. On the other hand, some Believers who attend a meeting where a few may be genuinely slain in the Spirit may feel that if they do not fall, others will think them unspiritual or resisting the move of the Spirit. I am here to tell you that a "courtesy fall" is never the work of the Holy Spirit.

Slain in the Spirit:
The phrases "slain in the Spirit," "falling under the power," or "soaking or resting in the Spirit" are not found anywhere in the

Bible. They are used, however, to describe the experience of falling to the floor under the power of the Holy Spirit. Although being slain in the Spirit seems to be a distinguishing characteristic of some recent revivals and evangelistic ministries, there are recorded accounts of people falling under the power of God or being slain in the Spirit in 18th and 19th century revivals. Some of the earlier recorded prostration experiences were however related to sinners falling under conviction for their sins. Let us explore a few Biblical examples of this phenomenon, which is sometimes referred to as "being slain in the Spirit" or "falling out under the power" or "soaking or resting in the Spirit":

"While I, Daniel, was watching the vision and trying to understand it, there before me stood one who looked like a man. [16]And I heard a man's voice from the Ulai calling, "Gabriel, tell this man the meaning of the vision." [17]As he came near the place where I was standing, I was terrified and fell prostrate. "Son of man," he said to me, "understand that the vision concerns the time of the end." [18]While he was speaking to me, I was in a deep sleep, with my face to the ground. Then he touched me and raised me to my feet." Daniel 8:15-18

"As he neared Damascus on his journey, suddenly a light from heaven flashed around him. [4]He fell to the ground and heard a voice say to him, "Saul, Saul, why do you persecute me?" [5]"Who are you, Lord?" Saul asked. "I am Jesus, whom you are persecuting," he replied. [6]"Now get up and go into the city, and you will be told what you must do." Acts 9:3-6

"On the Lord's Day I was in the Spirit, and I heard behind me a loud voice like a trumpet, [11]which said: "Write on a scroll what you see and send it to the seven churches: to Ephesus, Smyrna, Pergamum, Thyatira, Sardis, Philadelphia and Laodicea." [12]I turned around to see the voice that was speaking to me. And when I turned I saw seven golden lampstands, [13]and among the lampstands was someone "like a son of man," dressed in a robe reaching down to his feet and with a golden sash around his chest. [14]His head and hair were white like wool, as white as snow, and his eyes were like blazing fire. [15]His feet were like bronze glowing in a furnace, and his voice was like the sound of rushing waters. [16]In his right hand he held seven stars, and out of his mouth came a sharp double-edged sword. His face was like the sun shining in all its brilliance. [17]When I saw him, I fell at his feet as though dead. Then he placed his right hand on me and said: "Do not be afraid. I am the First and the Last. [18]I am the Living One; I was dead, and behold I am alive for ever and ever! And I hold the keys of death and Hades. [19]"Write, therefore, what you have seen, what is now and what will take place later." Revelation 1:10-19

These are just a few passages but all of them show that when someone falls under the power of either the Lord's Presence or that of the Angels of the Lord, they all fall on their faces. Also either during the time they are "slain" or upon their awakening there was most likely either an internal work that the Holy Spirit did in that life or a message or other direction was given. Whatever occurred at the end the Believer will know the purpose of the Lord and what needs to be accomplished.

And while my personal experiences may not count in some peoples' mind as valid proof for authenticating such a phenomena, I would still venture in revealing that I have fallen once in a public meeting when a Prophet of God began to prophesy over me. He did not touch me but I fell to my face as the word was being given and while being "slain in the Spirit" the Lord spoke to me very clearly about what He desired for me to do. There were other occasions when this has happened to me in my private prayer time and on every occasion I knew what transpired either during or after the occurrence!

Anytime there is a genuine move of God which may include manifestations of the Holy Spirit, this must always be welcomed in the Church of Jesus Christ as we are encouraged not to quench the Holy Spirit [1 Thessalonians 5:19]. However, we must be careful to keep our focus and desire on Jesus Christ rather than on any manifestation. Some Believers travel from church to church when they hear about weird and wonderful occurrences happening supposedly under the power of the Holy Ghost. They are thrill seekers with little depth and little discernment. In our seeking we must willingly obey God's Word in everything we do. Here is what the Scripture says concerning this:

> "Rejoice always, [17]pray without ceasing, [18]in everything give thanks; for this is the will of God in Christ Jesus for you. [19]Do not quench the Spirit. [20]Do not despise prophecies. [21]Test all things; hold fast what is good. [22]Abstain from every form of evil." [NKJV] 1 Thessalonians 5:16-22

The question then remains; how can we recognize true spiritual manifestations that are indeed prompted and controlled by the Holy Spirit? In the last decade, there was a preoccupation with gold dust falling, and with raucous laughter overtaking the meeting to name a few. In doing so we would need to answer the following questions! The bottom line is this: does Scripture back it up? Was Jesus Christ glorified and did it change lives? Is the Believer becoming more and more like Jesus Christ? Are the fruits of the Spirit—love, joy, peace, patience, gentleness, goodness, faith, meekness, and self-control, becoming more evident and increasing after a personal experience in the Presence of the Lord? Confirmation that a spiritual experience is real and Biblical lies in the fact that the Believer is growing into the Stature of Jesus Christ.

Another phenomena seen in today's Church is what is being called "drunk in the Spirit" I would like to quote from an article published by J. Lee Grady in the October 28, 2009 edition of Charisma magazine. Used by permission.

Getting "drunk in the Holy Spirit" has been a popular concept in some churches. But is it Biblical? – J. Lee Grady

A few years ago a traveling charismatic minister from the West coast passed through Florida to conduct a series of renewal meetings. I'd never heard of the guy, but the rumour was that he carried a "special" anointing. It was unique, that's for sure-especially when he took the microphone, slurred his words as if intoxicated and leaned to the left of the pulpit as if he were about to fall over. Then, in between some bizarre spasms, he would shout what sounded like "*Walla walla bing bang!*"

His message didn't make sense. But if he had just said "*Ding Dong Bell*" or "*Yabba Dabba Doo*" over and over, some people in his meetings would have run to the front of the room and swooned, even though he never opened his Bible during his message. They wanted what this man claimed to possess—an anointing to become "drunk in the Spirit." Spiritual intoxication has been a trend in charismatic circles for a while. Some respected preachers, citing Acts 2:13, defend the concept that Christians might feel drunk when they are filled with the Holy Spirit [because the early disciples were accused of being drunk when they spoke in tongues]. This teaching led to lots of disorderly conduct in revival meetings—including nosebleeds, bruises and more serious injuries.

Some people began to manifest what looked like seizures during renewal services, and the bizarre behaviour was defended as "manifestations of the Spirit." Some pastors even encouraged wobbly saints to find "designated drivers" if they felt too drunk to operate a vehicle when it was time to go home. Meanwhile, some worship leaders introduced "Holy Ghost drinking songs" that encouraged people to slosh around in the joy of the Lord while uncorking more of His new wine.

The spiritual drunkenness craze led to other charismatic fads, including an infatuation with angels, an obsession with golden dust and the strange teachings of John Crowder—a confessed "new mystic" who compares the infilling of the Holy Spirit to smoking marijuana.

Crowder, who is planting a church in Santa Cruz, Calif., this fall, sometimes calls his meetings "sloshfests" and refers to himself as a bartender for God. He teaches that God wants all Christians to be continually drunk in the Holy Spirit—and he provides resources to help you do just that, including an electronic recording that will help you, in Crowder's words, "trance out," and a teaching that encourages stigmata and levitation.

I'll let the theologians sort out all the obvious reasons why Crowder and other "new mystics" are treading on dangerous ground. Meanwhile I have a less complicated concern. With all of this emphasis on Holy Ghost intoxication, did anybody notice that the Bible clearly commands us to be spiritually *sober?*

If soberness wasn't mentioned in the New Testament, then I wouldn't be beating this drum so loudly. But I find numerous references, from both Apostles Peter and Paul. "But you, *be sober in all things*," is Apostle Paul's admonition to Timothy [2 Timothy 4:5, NASB]. He tells the Thessalonians, "But since we are of the day, *let us be sober*, having put on the breastplate of faith and love, and as a helmet, the hope of salvation," [1 Thessalonians 5:8].

Apostle Peter hammers the same point. He wrote, "Prepare your minds for action, keep sober in spirit, fix your hope completely on the grace to be brought to you at the revelation of Jesus Christ" [1 Peter 1:13] and "The end of all things is near; therefore, be of sound judgment and *sober spirit* for the purpose of prayer" 1 Peter 4:7.

The soberness here is not primarily a reference to abstaining from alcohol [although it's worth mentioning that believers who drink will find it more difficult to obey these commands]. To be sober can be defined "to show self-control," "to be sane or rational," or "to be free from excess or extravagance." A sober Christian knows the heights of God's inexpressible joy, but he is never ruled by emotions, passions, lust or any other category of temptation that has the power to dull the spiritual senses.

When I look at the state of our nation today, and consider our spiritual challenges, it's obvious the last thing we need are Christians who are so sloshed in emotional euphoria that they can't pray intelligently and work diligently.

This is not a time for God's people to be incapacitated. We need to be thinking, planning, strategizing, researching and building— all using the Holy Spirit's wisdom. Yes, we need to be filled with the Holy Spirit like never before—but He is not going to fill us so we can act like giddy freshmen at a frat house keg party. Let's put the childish things behind us. It's time for us to grow up and sober up. *"End of article"*!

I believe that the preceding article points to the very counterfeit operations of false apostles and false ministers masquerading in the Church today that need to be exposed.

Drunk In The Spirit:
The Scripture used to back up this practice is found in Acts 2:13 which says: "Others joked, "They're drunk on cheap wine."" [MSG]

All Scripture needs to be interpreted rightly by using exegesis [finding the meaning of the text which then leads to discovering its significance or relevance]. Many interpret the Scriptures using eisegesis [the interpretation of a text by reading into it one's own ideas – thus misinterpreting it] in order to have Scripture back up the behaviour they are trying to pass off as God-ordained. In laymen's terms, we must allow the Scriptures to determine our doctrine and form the basis for our experiences and not the other way around of making our doctrine and experiences determine the Scriptures.

If a person drinks alcohol, it eventually intoxicates them and the person will go into an intoxicated stupor. They may not have control of themselves. Some very mild-mannered people when drunk become aggressive, combative people. The baptism in the Holy Ghost comes upon a person and there may be some feelings of euphoria as He baptizes with rivers of love, and the person might be totally overwhelmed by His Presence, but you remain conscious with full control of your emotions and actions. The Holy Spirit does not produce drunkenness in the same way that a bottle of Jack Daniels or Johnny Walker does.

In interpreting the manifestation that occurred when the Holy Spirit arrived on the Day of Pentecost, we need to carefully note what the Scriptures actually said and did not say.

- They were all filled with the Holy Spirit.

- This infilling with the Holy Spirit was evidenced by them

all speaking in tongues that they obviously did not learn or spoke in before.

- It said that there were mockers in verse 13 attempting to make fun of the Apostles, and discredit them and the others by saying that they were drunk with some sort of new, cheap wine.

- They were deemed incoherent by the scoffers due to the noise they made as they spoke in other tongues. They sounded incoherent because they were all speaking in languages that they did not learn. This was completely new to all who witnessed this phenomenon.

- In responding to these mockers, Apostle Peter stood and boldly proclaimed that they were not drunk!

Noteworthy in this instance is the fact that the mockers who witnessed the Upper Room event of the baptism in the Holy Spirit are the ones who stated "They have had too much wine." [Acts 2:12]. It has since become popularly known as "drunk in the Spirit." It was not the Apostles sayings such things! Apostle Peter boldly proclaimed a little further on... "[15]These men are not drunk, as you suppose. It's only nine in the morning!" The Holy Spirit was using them to establish the foundation of the Church!

The other text of Scripture that is used in support of this drunken behaviour by many today is found in the Apostle Paul's letter to the Ephesians church where he writes:

> "Do not get drunk on wine, which leads to debauchery. Instead, be filled with the Spirit. [19]Speak to one another with psalms, hymns and spiritual songs. Sing and make music in your heart to the Lord, [20]always giving thanks to God the Father for everything, in the name of our Lord Jesus Christ." Ephesians 5:18-20

Once again in this passage the Apostle Paul is contrasting drunkenness with the infilling of the Holy Spirit and is no way suggesting that when one is filled with the Holy Spirit that, that person enters into "holy debauchery" [debauchery – extreme indulgence in sensuality]. He was saying that in the same manner that some are drunk and are under the influence of alcohol, let the Believers in the Lord Jesus Christ come under the influence of the Holy Spirit!

I believe that there is a marked difference between someone who is intoxicated from the excessive consumption of alcohol and one who is filled with the Holy Spirit. The person who is drunk from alcohol is not in control of their actions while the Spirit-Filled Believer is in control of their actions guided by the Holy Spirit!

Here the Apostle Paul is saying that while being drunk from the influence of excessive alcohol leads to debauchery and excess; being filled with the Holy Spirit should produce a life marked by encouragement to fellow Believers, the making of melody to the Lord within the heart and the giving of thanks to the Father, in the Name of Jesus Christ!!!

Once again I think we need to ask this very sobering question: Is being "drunk in the spirit" really a blessing? Should it even be spoken of in this light?

There is so much more that can be written about the leaven of the Corinthians, that this book will not be able to contain. However, there is one other aspect about this leavening effect that I would like to highlight and that is sexual immorality in the Church.

Remember that the city of Corinth was utterly immoral and one indication of this was the hotspot of the day -- the temple of Venus [Aphrodite] that hosted 1000 priestesses dedicated to prostitution in the name of religion.

The Apostle Paul had to address the issue of sexual impurity in the church when he wrote: "It is actually reported that there is *sexual immorality* among you, and such *sexual immorality* as is not even named among the Gentiles--that a man has his father's wife!" [1 Corinthians 5:1]

Sexual sin is still rampant in today's Church from the top down, as we hear of reports of many un-Scriptural divorces, as well as homosexuality, incest, rape, lesbianism etc. Don't get me wrong, there are valid reasons for divorce, but divorce among leaders in the Church, especially here in North America is becoming an epidemic and we need to shout it from the roof top that it is wrong and must cease. Here is an excerpt from my just published book "I Will Build My Church. – Jesus Christ" on this issue[15]:

Divorce and Remarriage amongst Leaders!
The epidemic of divorce and remarriage among leaders within the ranks of professing Christian ministries, especially here in North America are somewhat disconcerting. When leaders divorce their Bible-believing, Born-again spouses and then re-marry and their spouses are still serving Christ, this is unacceptable behaviour and very unscriptural. This practice actually glorifies the spirit of antichrist...

Marriage is a very, very serious matter with the Lord as it speaks directly to Jesus Christ and His Church [Bride]. As a matter of fact life as we know it began with a marriage [Adam and Eve] and will end with a Marriage [Jesus Christ and His Church – His Bride]! Marriage among Believers was never intended to end in divorce and as such we must examine this issue very carefully as some may be rudely awakened when they come face to face with the Lord! As a pre-cursor to what I am about to say; here is what the Lord said:

> "It has been said, 'Anyone who divorces his wife must give her a certificate of divorce.' [32]But I tell you that anyone who divorces his wife, except for marital unfaithfulness, causes her to become an adulteress, and anyone who marries the divorced woman commits adultery." Matthew 5:31-32

Given the present North American culture in which we live this Scripture could easily be read – "*It has been said, 'Anyone who divorces his or her spouse must give a certificate of divorce.' [32] But I tell you that anyone who divorces his or her spouse, except for marital unfaithfulness, causes him or her to become an adulterer or adulteress, and anyone who marries the divorced man*

---

[15] Ordering details to the aforementioned book can be found at the end of this book!

ɔr woman commits adultery." [Author's interpretation]

Apostle Paul writing by the Holy Spirit also gives a very stinging piece of advice and direction to the Church, when he wrote:

> "To the married I give this command (not I, but the Lord): A wife must not separate from her husband. [11]But if she does, she must remain unmarried or else be reconciled to her husband. And a husband must not divorce his wife. [12]To the rest I say this (I, not the Lord): If any brother has a wife who is not a believer and she is willing to live with him, he must not divorce her. [13]And if a woman has a husband who is not a believer and he is willing to live with her, she must not divorce him. [14]For the unbelieving husband has been sanctified through his wife, and the unbelieving wife has been sanctified through her believing husband. Otherwise your children would be unclean, but as it is, they are holy. [15]But if the unbeliever leaves, let him do so. A believing man or woman is not bound in such circumstances; God has called us to live in peace. [16]How do you know, wife, whether you will save your husband? Or, how do you know, husband, whether you will save your wife? [17]Nevertheless, each one should retain the place in life that the Lord assigned to him and to which God has called him. This is the rule I lay down in all the churches." 1 Corinthians 7:10-17

In the early Church, the question of divorce and remarriage among Church leaders [Apostles, Prophets, Evangelists, Pastors, Teachers, Elders and Deacons] was very seldom raised but it was addressed nonetheless as it undoubtedly occurred among the Saints. Today, however, it has become a significant problem in evangelical Christian circles among leaders. Infidelity is no longer a rare occurrence, and it is indeed sad to see and hear that almost weekly that there is news of yet another new "affair" from leaders in the Church. With such examples in the leadership, undoubtedly it is safe to assume that it must be even more common among the general membership.

I would like to go on record and categorically state that the divine standard for marriage is the lifelong commitment to one's spouse, and nothing else! At the time of Jesus Christ's existence on earth even though the Old Testament was in effect and divorce was permitted in some cases under the Old Testament economy, He made it absolutely clear that divorce was not God's ideal. As a matter of fact the Pharisees posed the very question regarding marriage to Jesus as recorded in Matthew:

> "Some Pharisees came to him to test him. They asked, "*Is it lawful for a man to divorce his wife* for any and every reason?" [4]"Haven't you read," he replied, "that at the beginning the Creator `made them male and female,' [5]and said, `For this reason a man will leave his father and mother and be united to his wife, and the two will become one flesh'? [6]*So they are no longer two, but one. Therefore what God has joined together, let man not separate.*" [Italics added] Matthew 19:3-6

Jesus Christ went on to qualify His statement in light of their question so that there could be no confusion whatsoever. Remember that these Pharisees wanted to be able to divorce for any reason they seem fitting [just like so many leaders today]! Here is what He said in response to the Pharisees:

> "*Then, why,*" they asked, "*did Moses say a man may divorce his wife by merely writing her a letter of dismissal?*" [8]Jesus replied, "Moses did that in recognition of your hard and evil hearts, *but it was not what God had originally intended.* [9]And I tell you this, that *anyone who divorces his wife, except for fornication, and marries another commits adultery.*" [Italics added TLB] Matthew 19:7-9

Again Jesus made it absolutely clear as to the standard concerning marriage and divorce in the writings of both Apostles Luke and Mark. To Him, this must be of paramount importance seeing He is the Builder of His Church and it is recorded a number of times!

> "Anyone who divorces his wife and marries another woman commits adultery, and the man who marries a

divorced woman commits adultery." Luke 16:18

"When they were in the house again, the disciples asked Jesus about this. [11]He answered, "Anyone who divorces his wife and marries another woman commits adultery against her. [12]And if she divorces her husband and marries another man, she commits adultery." Mark 10:10-12

In both these cases, Jesus Christ explicitly warned that remarriage after divorce amounts to adultery, a sin which is forbidden by God. Both divorce and remarriage are extremely serious steps, and both violate the divine principle of the permanent union and faithfulness in marriage.

Even though extramarital sex would indeed create severe problems in a marriage that would allow divorce, God's ideal is to forgive the indiscretions so long as it is accompanied by genuine repentance and a renewed faithfulness. There may still be a solid foundation for a good marriage if the person is able to forgive the erring partner. I am not saying that it is easy, but it is the high road. If the innocent partner cannot forgive the cheating partner, then due to the fornication aspect of the extra-marital affair, divorce is permitted.

However, we must remember that leaders must be held to a higher standard and these issues should not even arise among those who assume leadership positions in the Church; both Universal and local. The qualifications for Biblical, Church leadership have been clearly spelt out!

Elders, Overseers or Bishops:
"An elder must be blameless, the husband of but one wife, a man whose children believe and are not open to the charge of being wild and disobedient." Titus 1:6

And in Timothy 1 Timothy 3:2-3 we read.
"Now the overseer must be above reproach, the husband of but one wife, temperate, self-controlled, respectable, hospitable, able to teach, [3]not given to drunkenness, not violent but gentle, not quarrelsome, not a lover of money.

Deacons:

> "A deacon must be the husband of but one wife and must
> manage his children and his household well." 1 Timothy 3:12

Popular opinion may dictate one thing but the Word of God is as
clear and as plain as you can get it – marriage, divorce and
remarriage among Believers, especially those in leadership is not
God's way! The first course of action for any such deviant
behaviour as fornication or adultery is for repentance, forgiveness
and reconciliation. If that does not work, divorce is acceptable
and if the innocent partner remarries they are free from
committing adultery! If the offending partner leaves the marriage
and remarries then they are living in adultery. And this is what
the Bible says about adulterers and adulteresses:

> "Do you not know that the wicked will not inherit the
> kingdom of God? Do not be deceived: Neither the
> sexually immoral nor idolaters nor adulterers nor male
> prostitutes nor homosexual offenders [10]nor thieves nor the
> greedy nor drunkards nor slanderers nor swindlers will
> inherit the kingdom of God." 1 Corinthians 6:9-10

I have taken the liberty to spell out the varying reasons of divorce
and why it is or is not permitted. The Corinthian church was so
far gone that Apostle Paul has to address a situation in the church
where a man was having sexual intercourse with his step-mother
[his father's wife]. This was akin to incest and Apostle Paul was
very deliberate and direct in his divinely directed instructions!

> "I wrote unto you in an epistle not to company with
> fornicators: [10]Yet not altogether with the fornicators of this
> world, or with the covetous, or extortioners, or with
> idolaters; for then must ye needs go out of the world.
> [11]But now I have written unto you not to keep company,
> if any man that is called a brother be a fornicator, or
> covetous, or an idolater, or a railer, or a drunkard, or an
> extortioner; with such an one no not to eat. [12]For what
> have I to do to judge them also that are without? do not
> ye judge them that are within? [13]But them that are without

God judgeth. Therefore put away from among yourselves that wicked person." [KJV] 1 Corinthians 5:9-13

In the Book of Revelation as Apostle John wrote what the Lord had given to him for the Church, he spoke quite a bit about fornication in Revelation 2:14, and in Revelation 2:20-23.

Sexual sin of any kind is wrong and must be purged out of the Church of Jesus Christ as we move towards a place of maturity. As we close this chapter on the leaven of the Corinthians here is what I consider to be the full list of ills that plagued that church and that we need to be aware of:

- There were divisions, personality cults, cliques and endless quarrels amongst the members – 1 Corinthians 1:10-11

- Carnality and envy outweighed their spirituality – 1 Corinthians 3:3

- They sought after worldly wisdom and materialism and were very proud – 1 Corinthians 3:19

- The church was filled with all kinds of sexual immorality – 1 Corinthians 5:1

- Because of their selfish pride, they had no interest in removing sin from their church – 1 Corinthians 5:2 – There was a failure to discipline members who had fallen into sin.

- The church was filled with arrogance – 1 Corinthians 5:2

- Rather than forgive one another, they took each other to court – 1 Corinthians 6:6-8

- Sexual perversion, fornication, incest, and adultery were commonly practiced, as many members did not honour their marriage vows – 1 Corinthians Chapter 7

- They were idolatrous – 1 Corinthians 10:14

- The church tolerated wrong doctrines – 1 Corinthians 11:19

- They partook of the Lord's Supper in a selfish and unworthy manner – 1 Corinthians 11:21-30

- They coveted one another's spiritual gifts – 1 Corinthians 12

- They showed no interest in witnessing to any unbelievers that might be present – 1 Corinthians 14:23

- They shouted over each other, not listening to what one another had to say – 1 Corinthians 14:26

- Some members felt they were above the Word of God – 1 Corinthians 14:36

- There was disorder in the church services – 1 Corinthians 14:40

- There were also heresies concerning the resurrection – 1 Corinthians Chapter 15.

Well, we have looked at the 5 types of bad leaven the Lord warned us about, namely:

The leaven of the Pharisees

The leaven of the Sadducees

The leaven of the Galatians

The leaven of Herod

The leaven of the Corinthians

Up to now, this has been an exposé on the evil and debilitating types of leaven. But there is one type that is to be pursued, that should be encouraged to thrive and we are encouraged to thrive and flourish in our lives. The leaven in question here is the Leaven of the Kingdom of Heaven. And I dare say that if allowed to, it can counteract and eliminate any effects of the bad leaven, as we shall see in the next chapter.

CHAPTER 9

THE LEAVEN OF THE KINGDOM

When we speak of the Kingdom of God what exactly are we referring to? Some people think it refers to heaven and the hereafter, but according to Romans it says:

"For the kingdom of God is not a matter of eating and drinking, but of righteousness, peace and joy in the Holy Spirit..." Romans 14:17

To qualify just what the Kingdom was and is, Jesus Christ while speaking to the multitudes by way of a parable interrupted His teaching and declared:

"The kingdom of heaven is like yeast that a woman took and mixed into a large amount of flour until it worked all through the dough." Matthew 13:33

In this final reference to leaven in the New Testament there has been some debate as to the true meaning of the Leaven of the Kingdom. Up to now, the other references to leaven have been symbolic of corrupting influence.

Jesus Christ warned of "the leaven of the Pharisees and the Sadducees", which included their teaching and hypocrisy.

Apostle Paul wrote of the danger of how "a little leaven leavens the whole lump", as he addressed the corrupting influence of sexual immorality, malice and wickedness and wrong doctrine. He also warned about the leaven of the Galatians which was folly, legalism or salvation by works rather than trusting in the

Grace of God. It also represents religiosity, walking in the flesh rather than the Spirit, being bewitched and turning away from "Present Truth[16]"! Jesus Christ also addressed the leaven of Herod which was malice, deceit and political guile. This has led some to conclude that "Leaven" spoken of in the parable of the Kingdom represents something evil.

However, there are several reasons why the Leaven spoken of here cannot represent an evil influence. Permit me once again to remind us that, we need to understand that all Scripture needs to be interpreted rightly by using exegesis [finding the meaning of the text which then leads to discovering its significance or relevance]. Many interpret the Scriptures using eisegesis [the interpretation of a text by reading into it one's own ideas – thus misinterpreting it]. In laymen's terms, we must allow the Scriptures to determine our doctrine and form the basis for our understanding and experiences and not the other way around of making our doctrine, understanding and experiences determine the Scriptures.

I believe that chief among the reasons as to why the Leaven of the Kingdom cannot be referring to any corrupting influence is the fact that the Kingdom that was preached so radically is the one that is now being declared, should it have been contaminated, it would have been destined to fail! We know this isn't so as the Kingdom is added to daily with the saving of souls that come to Jesus Christ. Another thing we should also take into consideration is whether leaven has ever been recognized in Scripture in the life of the Israelites in an acceptable way. And the answer to that is an unequivocal yes!

> "And the Lord spoke to Moses, saying, [10]"Speak to the children of Israel, and say to them: 'When you come into the land which I give to you, and reap its harvest, then you shall bring a sheaf of the firstfruits of your harvest to the priest. [11]He shall wave the sheaf before the Lord, to be accepted on your behalf; on the day after the Sabbath the

---

[16] For a more comprehensive understanding of "Present Truth" see the author's book – "Five Pillars of the Apostolic" ISBN 0-9686896-0-4

priest shall wave it. [12]And you shall offer on that day, when you wave the sheaf, a male lamb of the first year, without blemish, as a burnt offering to the Lord. [13]Its grain offering *shall be* two-tenths *of an ephah* of fine flour mixed with oil, an offering made by fire to the Lord, for a sweet aroma; and its drink offering *shall be* of wine, one-fourth of a hin. [14]You shall eat neither bread nor parched grain nor fresh grain until the same day that you have brought an offering to your God; *it shall be* a statute forever throughout your generations in all your dwellings. [15]'And you shall count for yourselves from the day after the Sabbath, from the day that you brought the sheaf of the wave offering: seven Sabbaths shall be completed. [16]Count fifty days to the day after the seventh Sabbath; then you shall offer a new grain offering to the Lord. [17]You shall bring from your dwellings two wave *loaves* of two-tenths *of an ephah. They shall be of fine flour; they shall be baked with leaven. They are* the firstfruits to the Lord. [18]And you shall offer with the bread seven lambs of the first year, without blemish, one young bull, and two rams. They shall be *as* a burnt offering to the Lord, with their grain offering and their drink offerings, an offering made by fire for a sweet aroma to the Lord. [19]Then you shall sacrifice one kid of the goats as a sin offering, and two male lambs of the first year as a sacrifice of a peace offering. [20]The priest shall wave them with the bread of the firstfruits *as* a wave offering before the Lord, with the two lambs. They shall be holy to the Lord for the priest. [21]And you shall proclaim on the same day *that* it is a holy convocation to you. You shall do no customary work *on it. It shall be* a statute forever in all your dwellings throughout your generations." [Italics in verse 17 added] Leviticus 23:9-21

Remember that Jesus Christ turned many traditional teachings upside down when He confounded the Priests and the Scribes by rescinding such popular teachings as an 'eye for an eye' by stating that love was the better way. He also told His disciples they must drink His Blood and eat His Flesh in order to have eternal life. This was perhaps a bit unsettling to those who thought of it literally.

I like what William Barclay, the renowned author, radio and television presenter, Church of Scotland minister and Professor of Divinity and Biblical Criticism at the University of Glasgow, had to say about this:

"In Jewish language and thought, leaven is almost always connected with an evil influence... It may well be that Jesus chose this illustration of the Kingdom deliberately. There would be a certain shock in hearing the Kingdom of God compared to Leaven; and the shock would arouse interest and rivet attention, as an illustration from an unusual and unexpected source always does.

The whole point of the parable lies in one thing – the overwhelming power of the Leaven. Leaven changed the character of a whole baking. The introduction of the Leaven causes a transformation in the dough; and the coming of the Kingdom causes a transformation in life.[17]

So now the obvious question that should be then asked is this: if Jesus Christ does not mean to use "Leaven" in this context as symbolical of a corrupting influence, then what does He mean?

To answer this question, I point you to the first time the Kingdom of God was spoken of in detail in Scripture in the Book of Daniel.

We need to remember that there are two kingdoms operating in the world: The Kingdom of God and the kingdom of satan or darkness! In light of this, I would like to re-visit king Nebuchadnezzar's dream and its interpretation as it reveals some very pertinent information concerning these two kingdoms and the eventual outcome. Daniel is considered as one the most accurate of all end-time Prophets, and while he and his fellow Israelites were captive in Babylon, the God of Heaven caused king Nebuchadnezzar to have a dream which he could not remember, let alone have it interpreted. The Lord then revealed

---

[17] William Barclay – The Gospel of Matthew, Volume 2, page 79

both the dream and its interpretation to Daniel and it pertained to the kingdoms of this world and the debilitating effect/influence by the Kingdom of God on them! Let's read the following account:

> "You, O king, were looking and behold, there was a single great statue; that statue, which was large and of extraordinary splendour, was standing in front of you, and its appearance was awesome. [32]"The head of that statue was made of fine gold, its breast and its arms of silver, its belly and its thighs of bronze, [33]its legs of iron, its feet partly of iron and partly of clay. [34]"You continued looking until a stone was cut out without hands, and it struck the statue on its feet of iron and clay and crushed them. [35]"Then the iron, the clay, the bronze, the silver and the gold were crushed all at the same time and became like chaff from the summer threshing floors; and the wind carried them away so that not a trace of them was found. But the stone that struck the statue became a great mountain and filled the whole earth. The Interpretation -- Babylon the First Kingdom [36]"This was the dream; now we will tell its interpretation before the king. [37]"You, O king, are the king of kings, to whom the God of heaven has given the kingdom, the power, the strength and the glory; [38]and wherever the sons of men dwell, or the beasts of the field, or the birds of the sky, He has given them into your hand and has caused you to rule over them all. You are the head of gold. Medo-Persia and Greece [39]"After you there will arise another kingdom inferior to you, then another third kingdom of bronze, which will rule over all the earth. Rome [40]"Then there will be a fourth kingdom as strong as iron; inasmuch as iron crushes and shatters all things, so, like iron that breaks in pieces, it will crush and break all these in pieces. [41]"In that you saw the feet and toes, partly of potter's clay and partly of iron, it will be a divided kingdom; but it will have in it the toughness of iron, inasmuch as you saw the iron mixed with common clay. [42]"As the toes of the feet were partly of iron and partly of pottery, so some of the kingdom will be strong and

part of it will be brittle. [43]"And in that you saw the iron mixed with common clay, they will combine with one another in the seed of men; but they will not adhere to one another, even as iron does not combine with pottery. The Divine Kingdom [44]"In the days of those kings the God of heaven will set up a kingdom which will never be destroyed, and that kingdom will not be left for another people; it will crush and put an end to all these kingdoms, but it will itself endure forever. [45]"Inasmuch as you saw that a stone was cut out of the mountain without hands and that it crushed the iron, the bronze, the clay, the silver and the gold, the great God has made known to the king what will take place in the future; so the dream is true and its interpretation is trustworthy." Daniel Promoted [46]Then King Nebuchadnezzar fell on his face and did homage to Daniel, and gave orders to present to him an offering and fragrant incense. [47]The king answered Daniel and said, "Surely your God is a God of gods and a Lord of kings and a revealer of mysteries, since you have been able to reveal this mystery." [Daniel 2:31-47 NASU]

In Daniel's interpretation of the dream he was declaring and revealing the colliding of world systems. He was revealing the intent of God's Kingdom for coming into the earth! There are a few things that I would like to highlight from Daniel's interpretation:

In king Nebuchadnezzar's dream he saw a "single great statue." The Hebrew word used to describe *great* here is the word "*saggiy*" and is rendered large in size and number but not great in terms of quality. In essence it is large and appears to be powerful but it has no substance – this is what the Kingdom of God will confront.

This is what the kingdoms of this world [cosmos – worldly systems] are really like. Also note that in king Nebuchadnezzar's dream the quality of this image is constantly diminishing in value. To the natural eye, the systems of this world may appear magnificent and astonishing at times but in reality they diminish in value and quality.

In contrast the Kingdom of God, [the stone cut out of the mountain] described in king Nebuchadnezzar's dream, "became A Great Mountain!" The Hebrew word used for *great* is the word *rab*; and is described as – superior in rank, internal capacity, and describes leadership – to stand at the top. Daniel spent time explaining the grandeur of the statue and then compares it to a mountain. God pays attention to substance on the inside and not external appeal. Someone looking at these two images [i.e. the statute and the mountain] in the natural without any divine revelation would easily choose the statue as its external appeal was much greater.

Daniel continued in his interpretation of the king's dream: "You continued looking until a stone was cut out without hands, and it struck the statue on its feet of iron and clay and crushed them." There was an impacting blow to the statue with no apparent source. The Kingdom of God is on a collision course with every system that bears the image of the statue. Every place this image is found it will be confronted!

The Kingdom, like Leaven, starts out small but continues until the King of the Kingdom rules. The Kingdom of God is highly confrontational. The Kingdom of God has the power to completely transform. The rock [representing the Kingdom of God] struck all entities [gold, silver, bronze, iron and clay] and they crumbled at the same time! The Kingdom of God will always prove itself to be superior to all world systems. That is the Greatness of The Kingdom of God!!!

This stone [representing the Kingdom of God] grew and grew until it "filled the whole earth" – not just certain structures in the earth – all the earth!

So to answer the question as to what Jesus Christ meant in referring to the Kingdom of God as Leaven:

He was saying:
As Leaven, the Kingdom of God will be very pervasive and would permeate and spread throughout the entire world.

He was also saying that just as Leaven is hidden in flour and seems insignificant, its effect soon becomes noticeable as the flour becomes affected by it. Just so shall the Kingdom of God operate until Its influence is in every sector of society, in every place in the earth!

Jesus Christ was also saying that in the same way leaven expands to every property of the flour mixture, the influence of the Kingdom of God would be complete. He declared that the entire loaf was completely leavened; there was no part of the loaf that remained unaffected. In like manner there will be no part of earth that will remain unaffected by the Kingdom of God.

In closing this book I would like to remind you of these words that Jesus Christ spoke:

> "Once, having been asked by the Pharisees when the kingdom of God would come, Jesus replied, "The kingdom of God does not come with your careful observation, [21]nor will people say, 'Here it is,' or 'There it is,' because the kingdom of God is within you." Luke 17:20-21

The Kingdom is not fleshly and physically satisfying. The Kingdom is a deep internal work of the Spirit of God that propels man to a place of perfection. It is the work of the Spirit in the heart of man. The Kingdom is a deliberate drawing down of spiritual values into the inner man. It does not come by observation. The Kingdom is the uncontested rule and Government of God that is established first in the heart of man then moves outwardly to all humans.

Remember that as Born-Again Believers in Jesus Christ, He stated emphatically and with great authority that the Kingdom of God is within us. So as we continue to allow the Kingdom to influence our lives the leaven of the Pharisees, Sadducees, Galatians, Herodians and/or the Corinthians will not be able to affect us. As the Leaven of the Kingdom continues Its work, we are being changed from glory to glory, and from strength to strength, complete into His very Image!!!

DOMINION-LIFE
INTERNATIONAL MINISTRIES

CANADA:
P.O. Box 44078 Kensington SQ
Burnaby, BC, V5B 4Y2
Canada

USA:
P.O. Box 1817
Ferndale, WA
98248, USA

TEL: 604-599-3542
FAX: 604-599-3543

Website:
http://www.dominion-life.org

Present-Truth Media

Website:
https://present-truthpublishing.com

OTHER EXCITING TITLES
By Michael Scantlebury

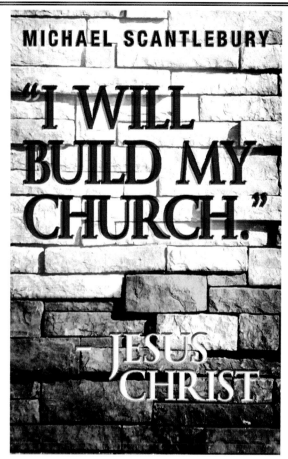

I WILL BUILD MY CHURCH. – JESUS CHRIST

"For we are his *masterpiece*, created in Christ Jesus for good works that God prepared long ago to be our way of life." Ephesians 2:10

What a powerful picture of the Church of Jesus Christ – His Masterpiece! Reference to a *masterpiece* lends to the idea that there are other pieces and among them all this particular one stands head and shoulders above the rest! This is so true when it comes to the Church that Jesus Christ is building; when you place it alongside everything else that God has created, The Church is by far His Masterpiece!

**For ordering details see the end of this book
Or visit www.wordalive.ca**

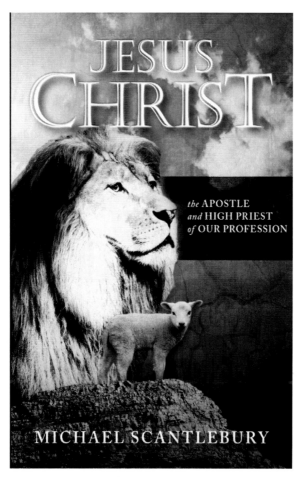

JESUS CHRIST THE APOSTLE AND HIGH PRIEST

There is a dimension to the apostolic nature of Jesus Christ that I would like to capture in His one-on-one encounters with several people during the time He walked the face of the earth and functioned as Apostle. In this book we will explore several significant encounters that Jesus had with different people where valuable principles and insight can be gleaned. They are designed to change your life!

FIVE PILLARS OF
THE APOSTOLIC

It has become very evident that a new day has dawned in the earth, as the Lord restores the foundational ministry of the Apostle back to His Church. This book will give you a clear and concise understanding of what the Holy Spirit is doing in The Church today!

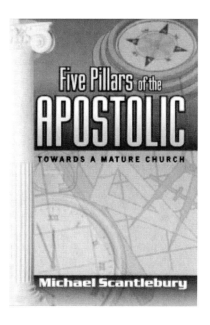

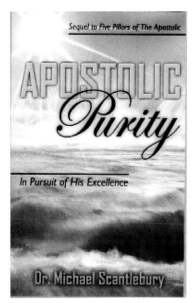

 ## APOSTOLIC
PURITY

In every dispensation, in every move of God's Holy Spirit to bring restoration and reformation to His Church, righteousness, holiness and purity has always been of utmost importance to the Lord. This book will challenge your to walk pure as you seek to fulfill God's Will for your life and ministry!

**For ordering details see the end of this book
Or visit www.wordalive.ca**

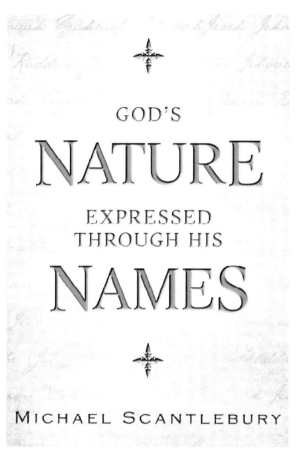

GOD'S NATURE EXPRESSED THROUGH HIS NAMES

How awesome it would be when we encounter God's Nature through the varied expressions of His Names. His Names give us reference and guidance as to how He works towards and in us as His people – and by extension to society! As a matter of fact it adds a whole new meaning to how you draw near to Him; and by this you can now begin to know His Ways because you have come into relationship with His Nature!

INTERNAL REFORMATION

"Internal Reformation" is multifaceted. It is an ecclesiology laying out the blue print of the Church Jesus Christ is building in today's world. At the same time it is a manual laying out the modus operandi of how Believers are called to function as dynamic, militant overcomers who are powerful because they carry internally the very character and DNA of Jesus Christ.

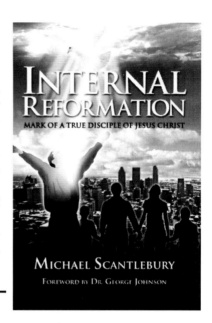

By Michael Scantlebury

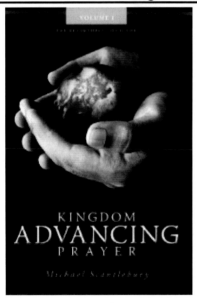

⇐ KINGDOM ADVANCING PRAYER VOLUME I

The Church of Jesus Christ is stronger and much more determined and equipped than she has ever been, and strong, aggressive, powerful, Spirit-Filled, Kingdom-centred prayers are being lifted in every nation in the earth. This kind of prayer is released from the heart of Father God into the hearts of His people, as we seek for His Glory to cover the earth as the waters cover the sea.

APOSTOLIC REFORMATION

If the axe is dull, And one does not sharpen the edge, Then he must use more strength; But wisdom brings success." [Ecclesiastes 10:10] For centuries the Church of Jesus Christ has been using quite a bit of strength while working with a dull axe [sword, Word of God, revelation], in trying to get the job done. This has been largely due to the fact that she has been functioning without Apostles, the ones who have been graced and anointed by the Lord, with the ability to sharpen.

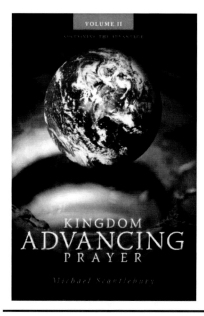

← **KINGDOM ADVANCING PRAYER VOLUME II**

Prayer is calling for the Bridegroom's return, and for the Bride to be made ready. Prayers are storming the heavens and binding the "strong men" declaring and decreeing God's Kingdom rule in every jurisdiction. This is what we call Kingdom Advancing Prayer. What a *Glorious Day* to be *Alive* and to be in the *Will* and *Plan of Father God*! *Hallelujah*!

By Michael Scantlebury

KINGDOM ADVANCING PRAYER VOLUME III

One of the keys to the amazing rise to greater functionality of the Church is the clear understanding of what we call Kingdom Advancing Prayer. This kind of prayer reaches into the very core of the demonic stronghold and destroys demonic kings and princes and establishes the Kingdom and Purpose of the Lord. This is the kind of prayer that Jesus engaged in, to bring to pass the will of His Father while He was upon planet earth.

For ordering details see the end of this book Or visit www.wordalive.ca

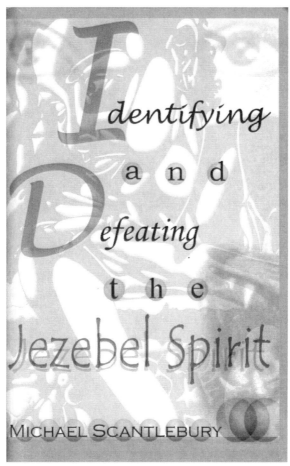

IDENTIFYING AND DEFEATING THE JEZEBEL SPIRIT

I declare to you with the greatest of conviction that we are living in the days when Malachi 4:5-6 is being fulfilled. Elijah in his day had to confront and deal with a false spiritual order and government that was established and set up by an evil woman called Jezebel and her spineless husband called Ahab. This spirit is still active in the earth and in the Church; however the Lord is restoring His holy apostles and prophets to identify and destroy this spirit as recorded in Revelation 2:18-23!

ORDER FROM
PRESENT TRUTH MEDIA
Orders please call 604-599-3542 |Fax 604-599-3543
Website – https://present-truthpublishing.com
Website – www.dominion-life.org

Ordering Information

Book Orders Please Contact:

Word Alive Press

In Canada/USA:
Phone: 866.967.3782 | Fax: 800.352.9272
International: Phone: 204.667.1400 | Fax: 204.669.0947
Website – www.wordalive.ca

Or From:
Present Truth Media

Phone: 604.599.3542 | Fax: 604.599.3543
Website – https://present-truthpublishing.com

Also Available From:
www.amazon.ca/com
www.chapters.Indigo.ca
www.barnesandnoble.com

MP3 SERIES BY
By Michael Scantlebury

APOSTOLIC RESOURCES:

Esther – Dynamics Of An Apostolic Church: Using Apostolic lenses, this revealing *7 part study* locates the destiny of the Church within the lives of Esther and her contemporaries, and decodes important patterns Churches and individuals alike need to follow as they are prepared to stand before the King.

Understanding The Kingdom Of God: In *19 messages*, Apostle Scantlebury provides an informative view into *The Kingdom and the Gospel of the Kingdom* that will equip and inspire you to become an active part in advancing God's Kingdom in the earth.

The Plumb Line: The Lord emphatically used the analogy of construction and a plumb line to provide principles the Body of Christ can use to inspect their current and future works to ensure that they match his specifications. This series will equip believers and churches alike to ensure that they meet God's building codes.

Cooperating With God's Nature: This extensive *35-part series* *explores* God meticulous revelation of Himself through the several Names He uses in the Bible, and gives us priceless clues that will equip us to interact and cooperate with Him on a deeper level.

Internal Reformation: In this *27-part series*, Apostle Scantlebury opens up the books of Ezra and Nehemiah, and the lives of the children of Israel, to reveal timeless principles of Internal change, and relates them to us in the 21st Century Church.

Apostolic Invasion Through The Life of Jesus Christ: This *16-part series* examines insightful ways Jesus functioned in His Apostolic anointing. Using several significant encounters, we unravel the technologies he used and the ways we can equip ourselves to walk as Jesus did.

CHURCH/LIFE BUILDING RESOURCES:

Restore Unto Me The Joy Of Your Salvation: Apostle Scantlebury handles this intimate request in a *five part series* that will help you understand what makes us lose our joy, what we need to do to reclaim it, and how we can never lose it again.

Negotiating Times Of Transition: In this compelling series, Apostle Scantlebury comforts and equips us to understand how we must navigate the God ordained process of transition in our lives, and gives us keys to win!

Understanding The Work Of The Holy Spirit: In this *five-part series*, Apostle Scantlebury takes a deep and fascinating look into the character and work of The Holy Spirit through enduring representations of Him in Scripture. You will be both blessed and empowered to live your utmost for His highest, as you follow with him in these teachings!

Exploring The Secrets Of Hidden Wealth: This unique *8-part series* will bless and astound you, as Apostle Scantlebury provides a clear, insightful analysis of what the Bible articulates concerning wealth and finances.

Non-Series Teachings: The teachings on this *two-volume set* include the following: Declaring Expansion | Defeating Discouragement | Defining Moments In Our Destiny | Real Discipleship | Dismantling A Nation's False Gods | Honour Key To Success | A Look At James 5 | Together Towards Our Destiny | People Of Reformation | Dealing With Failure | Reclaiming Lost Territory | Revisiting The Power Of Covenant | Sexual Promiscuity | Gold Seeker or Dirt Digger | Principles Of Deliverance, Transition And Change...

TO ORDER CONTACT:
PRESENT TRUTH MEDIA

Phone: 604.599.3542 | Fax: 604.599.3543
Website – https://present-truthpublishing.com
Website – http://www.dominion-life.org